MW00749025

CliffsNotes™

Investing for the First Time for Canadians

By Marguerite Pigeon
and Tracey Longo

IN THIS BOOK

- Invest successfully the first time
- Learn how to meet your investing goals
- Find investments that are right for you
- Track the progress of your investments
- Reinforce what you learn with CliffsNotes Review
- Find more investing information in CliffsNotes Resource Centre and online at www.cliffsnotes.com

CDG Books Canada, Inc.

CDG
BOOKS
CANADA

About the Authors

Marguerite Pigeon is an author and journalist whose titles include *Shopping Online For Canadians For Dummies* and the forthcoming *Investing In The Stock Market for Canadians*. She's worked as a writer, photographer, reporter, and producer for several news organizations including CTV and CBC Radio and CBC Television.

Tracey Longo has 15 years of journalism experience. She covers personal finance issues for national publications including *The Washington Post* and *Investor's Business Daily*. Her work has been regularly syndicated by *The New York Times*.

Publisher's Acknowledgements

Editorial

Senior Project Editor: Mary Goodwin

Acquisitions Editors: Joan Whitman, Mark Butler, Karen Hansen

Copy Editor: Liba Berry

Technical Editor: Joanne Follows, Investment Executive

Production

Project Coordinator: Donna Brown

Text Production: Kyle Gell Art & Design

Proofreader: Martha Wilson

Indexer: Wendy Thomas

CliffsNotes Investing for the First Time for Canadians

Published by
CDG Books Canada, Inc.
99 Yorkville Avenue
Suite 400
Toronto, ON M5R 3K5
www.cdgbooks.com (CDG Books Canada Web site)
www.cliffsnotes.com (CliffsNotes Web site)
www.idgbooks.com (IDG Books Worldwide Web site)

Canadian Cataloguing in Publication Data
Pigeon, Marguerite
    Investing fo the first time for Canadians

(CliffsNotes)
Includes index.
ISBN 1-894413-11-3

1. Investments — Canada. I. Longo, Tracey. II. Title. III. Series.
HG5152.P527 2000   332.67'8   C99-932652-X

Printed in Canada.

1 2 3 4 5 TRI 04 03 02 01 00

Distributed in Canada by CDG Books Canada, Inc.
For general information on CDG Books, including all IDG Books Worldwide publications, please call our distribution centre: HarperCollins Canada at **1-800-387-0117**. For reseller information, including discounts and premium sales, please call our Sales department at **1-877-963-8830**.
This book is available at special discounts for bulk purchases by your group or organization for resale, premiums, fundraising and seminars. For details, please contact our Special Sales department at **1-877-963-8830** or Email: spmarkets@cdgbooks.com.
For authorization to photocopy items for corporate, personal, or educational use, please contact Cancopy, the Canadian Copyright Licensing Agency, One Yonge Street, Suite 1900, Toronto, ON M5E 1E5; Tel: **416-868-1620**; Fax: **416-868-1621**; www.cancopy.com.

 is a trademark under exclusive license to CDG Books Canada, Inc. from International Data Group, Inc. in the United States and/or other countries.

CDG BOOKS CANADA

Table of Contents

INTRODUCTION

Welcome to the world of investing! It's an exciting world where you can make your money work for you. You can take your hard-earned cash and make it grow, helping you to achieve your financial goals, such as sending your children to university, living comfortably, and creating a secure retirement.

You can make all sorts of investments (for example, options trading, gas and oil ventures, collectibles, precious metals, futures, and real estate), but in this book we focus on some of the most common and accessible financial instruments.

With a little planning, almost everyone can get into investing. All you need is a set of firm goals and a little help to show you how you can best reach those goals. That's where this book comes in.

Why Do You Need This Book?

Can you answer yes to any of these questions?

- Do you need to learn about investing options fast?
- Don't have time to read 500 pages on investing?
- Are you unsure where to turn for simple, effective information on investing?
- Are you perplexed about exactly how to build an investment plan?

If so, then CliffsNotes *Investing for the First Time for Canadians* is for you!

How to Use This Book

The beauty of this book is that it takes the guesswork out of your decision making. It gives you the tools you need to identify your true financial goals, regardless of how lofty they may seem. Then you get crucial information on how you can meet those goals using the variety of investments that are available, including savings accounts, guaranteed investment certificates (GICs), registered retirement savings plans (RRSPs), stocks, bonds, mutual funds, and real estate, among others.

This book is designed to help you understand your investing choices on a fundamental level in light of your own goals, needs, and comfort level. Instead of wondering how different investment products work, CliffsNotes *Investing for the First Time for Canadians* gives you the fundamentals on the products that are available to you, what they can and can't do, what type of performance and risk you can expect, and how you can analyze investments to ensure that you select those that best meet your needs.

In addition, the book tells you where to turn for on-target, up-to-the-minute analysis and even provides you with a primer on how to get into each different type of investment.

You're the boss here. You get to decide how to use this book. You can either read the book from cover to cover or just look for the information you want and put it back on the shelf for later. However, we'll recommend a few ways to search for your topic(s):

■ Look for your topic in the table of contents in the front of the book.

■ Look at the In This Chapter list at the beginning of each chapter.

■ Flip through the book looking for your topic in the running heads at the top of the page.

■ Look for additional information in the CliffsNotes Resource Centre at the back of the book.

■ Use the index in the back of the book to find what you're looking for.

■ Or flip through the book until you find what you're looking for — because we organized the book in a logical, task-oriented way.

Also, to find important information quickly, you can look for icons strategically placed in the text. Here's a description of the icons you can find in this book:

■ When you see a Remember icon, make a mental note of this text — it's worth keeping in mind.

■ A Tip icon flags a helpful hint, a secret, or valuable advice.

■ A Warning icon alerts you to something that could be dangerous, requires special caution, or should be avoided.

Don't Miss Our Web Site

Keep up with the exciting world of investing by visiting the CliffsNotes Web site at www.cliffsnotes.com. Here's what you can find:

■ Interactive tools that are fun and informative

■ Links to interesting Web sites

■ Additional resources to help you continue your learning

At www.cliffsnotes.com, you can even register for a new feature called *CliffsNotes Daily,* which offers you newsletters on a variety of topics, delivered right to your e-mail inbox each business day.

If you haven't yet discovered the Internet and are wondering how to get online, pick up *Getting On the Internet,* new from CliffsNotes. You can learn just what you need to make your online connection quickly and easily. See you at www.cliffsnotes.com!

CHAPTER 1
SETTING REALISTIC GOALS AND EXPECTATIONS

In this chapter, you can learn about the starting points of thoughtful investing. You can also learn why you need to determine your goals and get started on your investment plan as early as possible.

Understanding Risk and Reward

What has drawn you to investing? Maybe it's the raging stock market of the 1990s. Or maybe you're enticed by the idea that you can put your money to work for you by investing it.

Although the benefits of investing are often made clear in success story after success story in advertisements, magazines, newspapers, and online Web sites devoted to investing, it's important to remember that there is no gain without potential pain. That means that when you invest your money, you can lose part or all of it.

Actually, rewards and risks are usually closely related. The greater an investment's potential for reward, the greater the potential for risk and actual loss. The high-flying stock that earned a 100% return last month is probably the very same stock that will tumble (and tumble hard) in the months and years ahead. The same goes for bonds and mutual funds and, potentially, even real estate.

You must take on some risk in order to reap the benefits of investing. That's the bad news. The good news is that sometimes, over time, a decent investment may bounce back and make investors whole again.

What's the best I can hope for?

The best you can hope to achieve with an investment depends on the nature of the investment. Some investments — such as savings accounts and GICs — offer stable, secure returns. Other investments — such as stocks, bonds, and mutual funds — depend entirely on market conditions. A *return* is an investment's performance over time. It's easy to calculate the best-case scenario with vehicles such as savings accounts, Canada Savings Bonds (CSBs) and GICs. On the other hand, you can never predict with 100% accuracy what kind of return you will get with more volatile investments such as stocks, bonds, and mutual funds.

You can, however, see how these investments have performed in the past. Recent history has many investors believing that the markets can only go up. If you look at returns on some stock investments, you can understand why.

For example, the top-performing stock on the Toronto Stock Exchange (TSE) in 1998, which was a technology company called Teklogix International Inc., racked up staggering returns of 463.1%. If you were lucky enough to invest $1,000 at the end of 1997, your money would have been worth $5,631 a year later. That's probably close to the best one-year return any investor can ever hope for — and then some.

The next-best-performing nine stocks on the TSE in 1998 returned between 135.2% and 440%, despite a mid-year market plunge. Because of that plunge, the best-performing stock mutual funds saw more moderate returns — between 1% and 14.9%. Long-term Government of Canada bonds brought in about a 15% return.

When evaluating what you can expect from investments like stocks, bonds, and mutual funds, a broad historical perspective is helpful. Long-term government bonds have fluctuated considerably since the 1950s, when returns were as low as 2% and 3% annually. In the 1980s those returns skyrocketed to more than 47%. But overall, the average annual return for long-term government bonds between 1950 and 1993 was a much more conservative 6.91%. T-bills, which are short-term debt issues (more on T-bills in Chapter 4), returned a 6.63% average in the same period, while corporate bonds were slightly better at 7.67%. Equities (stocks) have yielded the highest average annual return — about 11%, but have also tended to be more volatile. For investors who can't tolerate the risk of losing their initial principal, safer investments with lower returns might ultimately be the better choice. (Historical data from *Investments,* 2nd Canadian ed., Sharpe, Alexander, Bailey and Fower, Prentice Hall Canada 1997.)

What's the worst-case scenario?

You've heard about the best you can hope for, now what about the worst? The worst performer on the TSE in 1998 cost investors a frightening 86%. In other words, $1,000 would have been worth just $140 by the end of the year.

You can lose all of your money in an investment if a company declares bankruptcy.

What's a realistic course?

The good news is that if you try to choose your investments carefully — and subsequent chapters of this book give you the tools to do this — you should be able to minimize your losses. Ideally, your losses from any one investment may even be offset by the successes of your other investments.

Of course, if you're completely uncomfortable with the prospect of losing money, or if you need your money within five years, then investment vehicles such as stocks and bonds aren't for you. You're better off putting your money into safer, more liquid places such as bank accounts and guaranteed investments, discussed in Chapter 2, or in a money market mutual fund, explained in Chapter 3.

Realizing Gains through Compounding

Starting out as a first-time investor doesn't require a whole lot of money, which means that you don't need to wait until you've accumulated a large reserve of ready cash. You may ask: Why the big rush to start investing?

The answer is simple: You want to begin earning *compound interest* as soon as you can. Compound interest is actually the interest you earn on your interest. For example, if you invested $10,000 and earned 10% interest in the next year, your interest income would be $1,000. If you earned 10% again the following year, the $100 you would earn on the $1,000 (in interest you earned in the current year) would be considered compound interest.

Remember

Compounding is a compelling reason to start and keep investing for the long term because money left untouched reaps the greatest reward from compounding.

Table 1-1 shows you the power of compounding and how quickly even $100 saved or invested each month can grow under different interest rate scenarios.

Table 1-1:   The Beauty of Compound Interest

% Return	5 years	10 years	15 years	20 years	30 years
0%	$6,000	$12,000	$18,000	$24,000	$36,000
5%	$6,829	$15,592	$26,840	$41,275	$83,573
8%	$7,397	$18,417	$34,835	$59,295	$150,030
10%	$7,808	$20,655	$41,792	$76,570	$227,933
12%	$8,247	$23,334	$50,458	$99,915	$352,992

Tip

To calculate how many years it will take to double your money as a result of compounding, use the *Rule of 72*. Just follow these steps:

1. Determine what interest rate you think your money will earn.

2. Divide 72 by that interest rate.

The number you get is the number of years it will take to double your money.

For example, suppose that you believe you'll earn 8% annually in the coming years. If you divide 72 by 8, you can see that doubling your money will take nine years.

Focusing on a Goal

You can take the first step toward creating your investment plan by asking yourself a simple question: What do I want to accomplish? Actually, this step is your single most important move toward ensuring that your investment plan has a sound foundation. After all, these goals are the reason that you're launching a personal investment plan. So don't shirk this exercise. Dream away.

Perhaps you've always wanted to travel around the world or build a beachfront chalet. Or maybe you are interested in going back to school or starting your own business. Write down your goals. Your list of goals can serve as a constant reminder that you're on the course to success.

Don't forget the necessities, either. If you have kids who plan to go to college or university, you need to start preparing for that expenditure now. Your retirement plans fall into this category as well — now is the time to start planning for it.

Table 1-2 gives you a convenient format for writing down your goals. As you fill in Table 1-2, separate your goals into long-, mid-, and short-term time frames based on when you expect or need to achieve the goal. For example:

■ Buying a vacation home or retiring 10 or more years from now is a long-term goal.

■ Sending your child to college or university in 5 to 10 years is a mid-term goal.

■ Buying a car in the next 1 to 4 years because you know your current model is likely to be on its last legs is a short-term goal.

As you jot down your goals, also write down their costs. Use your best "guesstimate"; or if you're not sure, search the newspaper for, say, the cost of a beachfront home that approximates the one you want to purchase. Leave the "Time and Monthly Investment" category alone for now — that column represents the next step, which we tell you about shortly.

Table 1-2: My Goals

Time Frame	Cost	Time and Monthly Investment
Short-term:		
Mid-term:		
Long-term:		

Okay, now for the tricky part. How much do you need to invest each month, and over what period of time, to achieve your goals?

Of course, you need to know an approximate rate of return before you can plan. Your rate of return will differ, depending on the sort of investment you choose. Research can help you accurately estimate your rate of return. (Chapters 2, 3, and 4 tell you how to go about getting this information for different types of investments.)

As an example, Table 1-3 shows you what you need to invest each month to earn $100,000 over different periods of time.

Need $10,000 instead? Divide the monthly investment amount shown in Table 1-3 by 10. Want to save a million dollars instead? Simply multiply the amount by 10.

Table 1-3: Monthly Investments to Earn $100,000 at Varying Interest Rates

Years	5%	8%	10%
5	$1,480	$1,350	$1,280
10	$640	$540	$480
15	$370	$290	$240
20	$240	$170	$130

If you're older, in retirement, or just plain more conservative (and like keeping a good bit of your money in accounts or investments that earn less interest), you may want to use a lower estimated interest rate in your calculations to reflect your situation.

If you're investing in another type of asset — real estate, for example — a real estate agent in your area can tell you the appreciation rate or the annual rate of return for properties in your area. You can use that rate as a gauge to estimate what you're likely to earn in future years.

Tip

For determining how much you need to sock away annually to meet your goals over a specific period of time, using a scientific calculator is easiest.

Starting Your Savings Now

Throughout the rest of this book, we tell you about different types of investments that match your investment goals. To start out with any sort of investment, you need a cash reserve — and the amount varies, depending on your investment choice.

As you're doing your research and deciding which investments match your goals, start putting away $100 a month in an account earmarked for investment. By the time you determine the investing opportunities that best fit your needs, you should be well on your way to affording your investment.

Watching your dollars multiply can serve as motivation in itself: Your investment accounts may become as or more important to you than some of the other expenses that have eaten up your money in the past.

If you're the type who's been saving gobs of cash in a bureau drawer for a long time and now want to start earning real interest, you're one step ahead of the pack. You have the discipline. Now what you need is the knowledge and the tools.

The following chapters give you the tools you need to select investments and create an investment plan to meet all of your goals, including retirement. You also get the information you need to monitor your investments, so you can keep your plan on track.

CHAPTER 2
UNDERSTANDING SAVINGS, TIERED ACCOUNTS, AND GICS

IN THIS CHAPTER

- ■ Sticking with the tried-and-true: savings accounts
- ■ Tacking on more interest with tiered accounts
- ■ Discovering GICs

You can choose to be either a financial tortoise or a financial hare. As a financial hare, you can race ahead, spending everything you earn now, and have nothing later. Or, as a financial tortoise, you can pace yourself and spend responsibly, knowing that by spending a little less today, you can spend a lot more tomorrow. Assuming that you choose to be a financial tortoise, slowly and steadily socking away savings, where are you going to put those first dollars that you've set aside?

This chapter is about vehicles (investment options) that are appropriate for money that you don't want to put at great risk — for example, money that you have earmarked for emergency funds, or money that you're saving to buy a car, furniture, or a home within the next few years. By keeping your short-term money somewhere safe and convenient, you can feel comfortable putting your long-term money at somewhat greater risk. (Chapters 3 and 4 tell you about these kinds of riskier investments.)

Although they may not be the most exciting investments you'll ever make, savings accounts, tiered accounts, and GICs are worthwhile considerations for novice investors. Everyone should have some money in stable, safe investment vehicles. Savings accounts, tiered accounts, and GICs are basic savings tools and are the first step on your path to investing. These tools can help you build up the money that you need in order to start investing in other ways.

As you learn about investment vehicles through this book, you find out which ones are good for short-term investments and which are best for the long haul. How you invest your money depends largely on two factors: how long the money can remain out of your reach (time); and how much of it you can afford to lose (risk). Some investments are a lot riskier than others.

In this chapter, we tell you about the safest investments for short-term money that you can't afford to lose, and we also discuss what you need to know before you throw your hard-earned dollars into the pot.

Starting with Savings Accounts

Savings accounts are a form of investment — a very safe form. Although many banks don't pay interest on traditional chequing accounts, they almost always pay interest on traditional savings accounts. Most banks will offer a variety of accounts — some that combine an interest-bearing savings account with limited cheque-writing privileges.

For the most part, interest rates offered for traditional savings accounts differ only slightly from institution to institution. Don't expect too much. Today, the average savings account in Canada earns less than 1% daily interest. With this kind of return, it's no surprise more and more Canadians are choosing to sock money into slightly higher-yielding investments like money market mutual funds. (More on these in the section "Considering Different Types of Mutual Funds," in Chapter 3.)

When you further tack on inflation — even the very low rates seen in the past few years — that eats into your money over time, you might be asking yourself why you'd invest in a savings account at all.

There are several reasons to consider doing so. First, if you are a truly novice investor, a savings account can be the beginning of your learning process. You'll gain confidence when shopping around for the best possible interest rate, and again when you deal with the financial institution directly while opening the account.

Second, and more importantly, the money you invest in a savings account comes with an ironclad guarantee. Why? If the institution has Canadian Deposit Insurance Corporation (CDIC) insurance, your savings account is backed by the full strength and credit of the federal government. If the institution fails, the feds see that you automatically get your savings back — up to $60,000 per person, per institution, subject to some restrictions. As with any other insurance, you may sleep better knowing that it's there in the worst-case scenario.

Remember

Although putting your money in a savings account has serious limitations if it's your one and only investment strategy, having some of your money in a cash reserve makes sense. But as investments go, you wouldn't want to rely wholeheartedly on a savings account because the return on your investment is so low. Of course, factors such as fluctuating interest rates and the rate of inflation play a major role in how well your money does in this type of investment vehicle.

Chapter 6 gives you some guidelines for shopping around for a savings account. Make sure that you check out that chapter before calling a bank, trust, or credit union to ask about a savings account.

Web sites such as www.imoney.com publish lists of savings accounts interest rates at major Canadian financial institutions including banks, credit unions, and trusts.

Most banks charge a monthly or quarterly maintenance fee for a savings account. Some tack on an additional fee if your balance falls below a required minimum. In addition, you might be required to keep a savings account active for a specified time or face penalties.

Tiered Accounts

Some banks offer savings accounts with the added incentive of earning additional interest if your account balance remains consistently above a specified amount. This amount is usually at least $1,000, but it may be higher.

These types of accounts are often referred to as *tiered,* or as using *deposit interest tiers.* For example, according to the most recent interest rate structure, Scotiabank's "Scotia Gain Plan" account holders receive 1.15% interest on a minimum balance of $5,000 — almost a full percentage point higher than the bank's traditional daily interest savings account pays. At the Royal Bank, the "Royal Money-Maker Plus" account pays 1.15% interest on an account balance between $5,000 and $25,000. If you have between $25,000 and $60,000, that rate goes up to 2.35%, and increases again to 3.51% for accounts with anywhere from $60,000 to $100,000.

Some tiered accounts pay no interest at all on balances below a certain threshold. Find out whether that's a realistic sum for you before opening this type of account. Also, be sure to find out if the higher rates of interest apply to your entire balance or just the portion above the minimum needed to receive that rate. Finally, keep in mind that transaction fees for tiered accounts tend to be considerably heftier than you would face with a traditional savings account.

Considering Guaranteed Investment Certificates

If your savings grow to the point where you have more money than you think you need anytime soon, congratulations! One of the places you can consider depositing some of the balance is a guaranteed investment certificate (GIC).

A GIC is a receipt for a deposit of funds in a financial institution. Like savings accounts and money market accounts, GICs are investments for security.

With a GIC, you agree to lend your money to the financial institution for a number of months or years. You can't touch that money for the specified period of time without being penalized.

Why would a financial institution need you to loan it money? Typically, institutions use the deposits they take in to fund loans or other investments. If an institution primarily issues car loans, for example, it's apt to pay attractive rates to lure money to four-year or five-year GICs, the typical car-loan term.

Generally, the longer you agree to lend your money, the higher the interest rate you receive. The most popular GICs are for six months, one year, two years, three years, four years, or five years. There is no fee for buying a GIC.

By depositing the money (a minimum of $500 at most institutions) for the specified amount of time, the financial institution pays you a higher rate of interest than if you put your money in a savings or chequing account that offers immediate access to your money. When your GIC matures (comes due), the institution returns your deposit to you, plus interest.

The institution notifies you of your GIC's maturation by mail or phone and usually offers the option to roll the GIC over into another GIC. When your GIC matures, you can call your institution to find out the current rates and roll the money into another GIC, or transfer your funds into another type of account.

Some institutions give you a grace period, ten days or so, to decide what to do with your money when the GIC matures. In most cases, though, you can specify in advance what should happen to the money by giving your bank *instructions for maturation* when you buy the GIC. At a CDIC-insured financial institution, your investment is guaranteed to be there when the GIC matures.

You may have heard about investment vehicles called *term deposits.* Depending on the financial institution, term deposits function in almost exactly the same way as GICs. In some cases, these names are used interchangeably.

Financial advisers say that GICs make the most sense when you know that you can invest your money for one year, after which you'll need the money for some purchase you expect to make. The main reward of investing in GICs is that you know for sure what your return will amount to and can plan around it. That's because GIC rates are usually set for the term of the certificate. Be sure to check on the interest rate terms though, because some institutions change their rate weekly.

For example, after buying a house in early fall, our friend Mark made plans to have the exterior repainted the following spring (a short-term goal). In October, he received a nice $4,000 bonus from work. Knowing that he might be tempted to spend that money on dinners and CDs, Mark invested that $4,000 in a six-month guaranteed investment certificate with a 4.6% interest rate. When spring rolled around, his GIC matured, and he received $4,092. That amount he gained in interest may not sound like a lot, but it's more than four times as much as he would have received had he deposited the money in a typical savings account. And it's possibly $92 more than he would have had if he had kept the money in his regular, non-interest-bearing chequing account.

Refer to Figure 2-1 to see how much money you can make by buying a guaranteed investment certificate versus investing in a savings account.

GICs are most useful as an investment when interest rates are high, as they were back in the 1980s. These days, consistently lower interest rates mean Canadians should at least consider other types of investments that are both safe and will probably earn more money over the same period of time.

Figure 2-1: Comparing gains on a GIC versus a savings account, with an initial investment of $4,000.

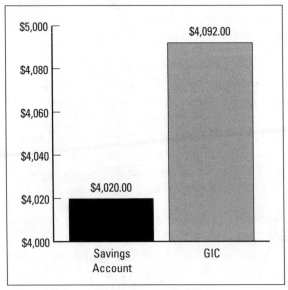

The interest rates paid on GICs are contingent on many factors. While they do tend to reflect prevailing interest rates in the general market, GICs have *administered rates,* meaning financial institutions use discretion when setting them. For example, banks may increase rates during RRSP contribution season to attract investors. This also means rates are negotiable, depending on the size of the deposit and the relationship between the bank and the client.

Because of this flexibility, it pays to shop around for GIC specials to get the best interest rate. Remember to check out the rates at credit unions too.

If you want your money back before the end of the GIC's term, you will be heavily penalized, usually with the loss of several months' worth of interest. A second drawback is that GICs are taxable. The principal, or the amount you originally invested, is considered income. As well, whatever interest you earn on your principal (including earnings from the market-linked GICs we discuss below) must be claimed as income, and is fully taxable on an annual basis. That means your financial institution will report the interest you earned during each tax year to Revenue Canada. You will pay tax on that amount annually — despite the fact that you won't see the interest until the GIC matures.

If rates are low, you may want to purchase shorter-term GICs and wait for rates to rise. This way, you won't be tying up your funds for long periods of time while rates might be climbing. As another option, some banks might allow you to add money to a GIC account at the interest rate of that particular day. The advantage to this method is that if you open the account on a day when the rate is low, you can increase your earnings by adding money at a higher rate, later.

Tip

Before you buy a traditional GIC or term deposit, ask about the relatively new *market-linked* GICs being offered by many of Canada's big financial institutions. Market-linked GICs are tied to the performance of the stock market. Like GICs, your principal is guaranteed. You won't lose any of your original investment, no matter how much the stock market fluctuates. But with a market-linked GIC, instead of receiving a fixed rate of interest, your return depends on the value of the stock market during the term of your deposit. If the stock market performs well, this will probably give you a bigger return than you could get with a traditional GIC — although most financial institutions will impose a maximum cap. If the market plummets, however, you might end up with the same amount you invested in the first place.

Turn to Chapter 6 for specific information on what questions to ask when shopping around for a GIC. See Table 2-1 for some suggested uses for entry-level investments.

Table 2-1:   The Uses for Entry-Level Investments

Type of Investment	Suggested Use
Savings Account or Tiered Account	Tuck away some money in a traditional or tiered chequing or savings account to allow you to access it quickly for emergencies, such as car repairs or dentist bills.
Guaranteed Investment Certificate (GIC) or Term Deposit	GICs and term deposits are good investments if you are saving for larger-ticket items such as a down payment on a car or a major appliance — items you don't intend to purchase for at least a year.

CHAPTER 3

UNDERSTANDING RRSPS AND MUTUAL FUNDS

IN THIS CHAPTER

- Finding out about RRSPs
- Mastering mutual funds

The investments discussed in this chapter are some of the most popular with Canadians — and the most useful. While in some cases your initial contribution isn't guaranteed the way it is in a savings account, the potential for growing your money is far superior. As well, mutual funds are managed by professionals, a fact that reduces the risk somewhat.

Investing in Registered Retirement Savings Plans

Established in 1957, RRSPs, or Registered Retirement Savings Plans, were designed by the federal government to help Canadians invest for retirement. Anyone who earns income (as defined by the government) can invest into an RRSP, and each of you should.

You set up your RRSP on your own, with a bank, mutual fund company or dealer, brokerage firm, credit union, trust company, insurance company or financial adviser. And you can invest your RRSP money in almost anything you can think of, from aggressive growth stocks to conservative GICs. You can own as many RRSPs as you want with a variety of institutions, but because you are often charged fees for each plan, it's wise to consolidate as much as possible.

Remember that long-term investments like those within an RRSP take advantage of long-term growth potential. That means, the earlier you start making contributions, the better. When you're in your 20s and 30s, retirement may seem impossibly far off — so far off, in fact, that it's hard to imagine planning for it now. However, if you want to retire in comfort, you have to think ahead.

Table 3-1 shows how financially beneficial it is to invest in an RRSP as early as possible. The first column shows the number of years before retirement the contributor started investing. The second column shows the accumulated balance at retirement, assuming annual contributions of $4,000 and an 8% annual return on investment.

Table 3-1: Investing Early for Retirement

Number of Years to Retirement	Accumulated Savings at Retirement
40 years	$1,123,124
30 years	$493,383
20 years	$201,691
10 years	$66,581
5 years	$29,343

Deciding not to contribute to an RRSP because you don't want to cut back on your take-home pay or telling yourself retirement is a long way off may prove to be a big mistake. Ultimately, you won't be paying yourself, and could risk ending up without enough money after you retire.

The key benefits of RRSPs

If you invest in an RRSP, your contributions offer two powerful, tangible benefits: First, an immediate tax deduction for the amount you've invested; and second, tax protection (a shelter) for the returns you will accrue on those investments within the RRSP until you withdraw the money at retirement.

Let's say, for example, that you earned $40,000 of taxable income this year, but made a $2,000 contribution to your RRSP. If your *marginal tax rate* (the highest rate of combined federal and provincial income tax you pay on the money you earn in a given year) is 40%, you will achieve an immediate tax savings of $800 for this year, bringing your tax bill down from $16,000 to $15,200. That's money you will now be able to spend or, even better, invest.

How much you can contribute

Your RRSP contribution limit depends on your earned income. You are allowed to contribute a percentage of that income every year, up to a maximum limit. As of 1999, the federal government allows you to contribute 18% of the tax year's earned income up to $13,500. The limit can be greater if you have a *carry-forward*, meaning that you contributed less than your limit in previous years. The limit goes down if you are also contributing to a company pension plan or participating in a Deferred Profit Sharing Plan.

Deciding where to put your RRSP money

A very broad range of investment vehicles is eligible to go into your RRSP, including the following that are discussed in this book:

- Deposits in savings or tiered savings accounts
- GICs and term deposits

- Stocks
- Bonds
- Mutual funds
- Mortgages

Depending on your risk tolerance, you can buy RRSPs that focus on different types of investments. *Guaranteed plans* invest in vehicles that guarantee you won't lose your principal, like GICs, and CDIC-insured savings accounts. With a guaranteed plan, you will know ahead of time exactly how much and how fast your money will grow. *Variable-rate plans* don't necessarily guarantee your initial investment, but can be very safe and offer far better returns. Those returns will fluctuate, however, since you can't predict the performance of the investment vehicles, like mutual funds or stocks. Keep in mind that with stocks and mutual funds, you have the added option of investing in a variety of fund types whose risk ranges from conservative to aggressive.

You don't have to choose just one kind of investment for your RRSP. In fact, unless your research tells you otherwise, you should invest only a certain percentage of your money in a high-risk investment, such as stocks. To determine what percentage of your money to invest in stocks, many financial advisers recommend that you subtract your age from 100. For example, if you're 25, you should invest 75% of your money in stocks.

When considering an overall investment portfolio, some financial planners advise using RRSPs for more conservative investments. The thinking here is that the tax-deferring power of your RRSP will compensate for lower returns. In other words, why jeopardize your retirement savings with high-risk investments when the real return on a more conservative RRSP investment may be only slightly lower?

Self-directed RRSPs

Most Canadians set up their RRSPs through a financial institution like a bank or mutual fund company. The institution puts your money into RRSP-eligible investment vehicles for you. Novice investors often choose this type of RRSP because they don't feel confident enough to do otherwise.

However, for those who want more control over their investment choices, you can set up what's called a *self-directed RRSP*, which allows you to pick and choose investment vehicles from wherever you want. Think of a self-directed RRSP as a shopping cart for the savvy investment consumer. Once you've chosen a particular investment, you place it in your cart to take advantage of the RRSP benefits discussed earlier.

You can register your self-directed RRSP with a financial institution or brokerage house, which becomes a trustee of the RRSP. In exchange, you may have to pay a yearly fee of about $125, although that fee is negotiable.

If you decide to set up a self-directed RRSP, you can transfer into it money you've already placed inside other RRSPs to create a single RRSP. To do so, you will have to fill out a special form provided by the federal government and pay a fee.

Even the savviest investment consumer needs advice. People with self-directed RRSPs should take advantage of the professional insights of a qualified financial planner to guide their strategy.

Spousal RRSPs

The government has made provisions within the RRSP system for spouses. The big advantage of a *spousal RRSP* is that it creates two separate sources of income, which generally results in tax savings when you retire. If one half of a couple earns a lot more money than the other, the spousal RRSP makes a lot of sense.

Let's say you are the higher earner. You set up a spousal RRSP in your spouse's name and contribute to it. In other words, you put in the money, but your spouse has legal control over it. Having done this, you reap two important benefits.

First, for every contribution, you will get a tax deduction (which will come in handy since you are being taxed at a higher rate on your higher income).

Second, and most importantly, when you have to withdraw money from the spousal RRSP at retirement, it will be taxed based on your spouse's lower income. Both of you benefit from a lower tax rate because the income has been split up, whereas all of the income would have been taxed at your higher rate if the money were coming solely out of your RRSP.

Contributing to a spousal RRSP does not preclude you from investing in your own RRSP, as long as the combined contribution does not exceed your allowable limit for that year.

Spousal RRSPs can actually lengthen the number of years you will be able to contribute to an RRSP past age 69. How? People over 69 are still allowed to put money into their partner's spousal RRSP until the year that person turns 69.

Foreign content inside RRSPs

While the Canadian economy is among the most stable in the world, domestic investments may not grow as fast as those in bigger and more powerful markets like the U.S., or emerging markets like those in the developing world. This fact has not escaped either investors eager to increase their returns or our federal government, concerned with fostering the

Canadian economy. The solution? The feds allow you to invest in foreign holdings inside your RRSP, but only up to a certain point. As of 1999, foreign investments can account for up to 20% of the *book value* of your RRSP. The book value is the exact dollar amount you've placed inside the plan — as opposed to the *market value,* which is the amount you could get if you cashed in the plan on any given day.

Borrowing from your RRSPs for a home or education

Most of the time, if you take money out of your RRSP before you retire, you pay income tax up front; what the government calls *withholding tax.* However, there are two instances in which the government lets you borrow from your RRSP tax-free and interest-free:

- **Home Buyer's Plan (HBP):** First-time home buyers (as defined by the federal government) can borrow up to $20,000 from their RRSP to finance their purchase through the HBP. This amount may double if you have a spouse with her or his own RRSP. However, the government has strict rules governing repayment, which must be completed within 15 years. Keep in mind, your HBP loan does affect the future gains you will miss out on for the period of time the money is outside your sheltered RRSP. For more on the HBP, see Chapter 9.

- **Lifelong Learning Plan (LLP):** Since 1999, people wanting to go back to school full-time to finish their education can borrow $10,000 per year up to a maximum of $20,000 over four years from their RRSP, using the LLP. The loan must be paid back within ten years. Like the HBP, your loan is interest-free and tax-free. But again, consider seriously the fact that the money you borrow will no longer be compounding inside your RRSP.

Borrowing for Your RRSP

While conservative investors may feel nervous about borrowing to put away money for their retirement, borrowing to make an RRSP contribution can be a smart option. Many lending institutions eager to attract clients towards their investment products will offer loans for very low interest rates. Also, because your RRSP contribution is tax-deductible, you will probably be eligible for a tax refund that can then be used to pay off a portion of your loan.

The interest you pay on an RRSP loan is not, unfortunately, tax-deductible.

Cashing in your RRSP and the benefits of RRIFs

Unless they are locked into a fixed-term investment, you can withdraw funds from your RRSP anytime. The government imposes no penalty for withdrawal. However, if you withdraw funds before the RRSP matures during the year you turn 69, you will be fully taxed on the money you take out — unless you are participating in the government's Home Buyer's Plan or Lifelong Learning Plan.

The government extracts the income tax on withdrawals up front through a withholding tax (simply the government's means of collecting the income tax right away). For more on withholding taxes, see the section "The price you pay for tapping your retirement accounts early," in Chapter 9.

As mentioned above, all RRSPs mature the year you turn 69. You have three options when you *convert,* or dismantle, your RRSP. They are:

- **Converting your RRSP into a lump sum cash payout.** By the end of the calendar year following your 69th birthday, unless you've made other arrangements, your RRSP funds must all be withdrawn and face combined federal and provincial income tax. This tax will be levied up front through the withholding tax, and can be very steep since it varies upward depending on the size of the withdrawal.

- **Convert your RRSP into an annuity.** People who want the security of knowing they will have a stream of income for the rest of their lives can choose to use their RRSP funds to buy a life *annuity*. Sold by insurance companies, many annuities pay regular instalments of fixed income for life. Annuities are not like investments that can grow or shrink. The payments are fixed and can pose problems because they are inflexible to factors like inflation.

- **Convert your RRSP into a Registered Retirement Income Fund, or RRIF.** This allows you to bypass some of the problems faced when choosing either of the preceding options. First, an RRIF will extend the benefit of the tax shelter by allowing you to withdraw your funds over time rather than in a highly taxed lump sum. Second, an RRIF gives you flexibility, since you maintain your investments, which can continue to grow — possibly earning you more money for the times in your retirement when you might need more. With an RRIF, you are required to withdraw a minimum amount each year (the first year you buy the RRIF is exempt from this minimum).

Defining Mutual Funds

A mutual fund is managed by an investment company that invests (according to the fund's objectives) in stocks, bonds, government securities, short-term money market funds, and other instruments by pooling investors' money.

Mutual funds are sold in shares. Each share of a fund represents an ownership in the fund's underlying securities (the portfolio).

Investors can sell their shares at any time and receive the current share price, which may be more or less than the price they paid.

When a fund earns money from dividends on the securities it invests in or makes money by selling some of its investments at a profit, the fund distributes the earnings to shareholders. If you're an investor, you may decide to reinvest these distributions automatically in additional fund shares.

Remember

A mutual fund investor makes money from the distribution of dividends and capital gains on the fund's investments. A mutual fund shareholder also can potentially make money as the fund's share per share (called *net asset value per share,* or *NAVPS*) increases in value.

```
NAVPS of a mutual fund = Assets
- Liabilities
÷ Number of shares in the fund
```

(*Assets* are the value of all securities in a fund's portfolio; *liabilities* are a fund's expenses.) The NAVPS of a mutual fund is affected by the share price changes of the securities in the fund's portfolio and any dividend or capital gains distributions to its shareholders.

Unless you're in immediate need of this income, which is taxable, reinvesting this money into additional shares is an excellent way to grow your investments, especially within your RRSP, where the gains you make will be sheltered from taxes.

Shareholders receive a portion of the distribution of dividends and capital gains, based on the number of shares they own.

As a result, an investor who puts $1,000 in a mutual fund gets the same investment performance and return *per dollar* as someone who invests $100,000.

Mutual funds invest in many (sometimes hundreds of) securities at one time, so they are diversified investments. A *diversified portfolio* is one that balances risk by investing in a number of different areas of the stock and/or bond markets. This type of investing attempts to reduce per-share volatility and minimize losses over the long term as markets change. Diversification offsets the risk of putting your eggs in one basket, such as technology funds. (See Chapter 8 for a detailed discussion of diversification.)

A stock or bond of any one company represents just a small percentage of a fund's overall portfolio. So even if one of a fund's investments performs poorly, 20 to 150 more investments can shore up the fund's performance. As a result, the poor performance of any one investment isn't likely to have a devastating effect on an entire mutual fund portfolio. That balance doesn't mean, however, that funds don't have inherent risks: You need to carefully select mutual funds to meet your investment goals and risk tolerance.

The performance of certain classes of investments — such as large company growth stocks — can strengthen or weaken a fund's overall investment performance if the fund concentrates its investments within that class. If the overall economy declines, the stock market takes a dive, or a mutual fund manager picks investments with little potential to be profitable, a fund's performance can suffer.

Unfortunately, unless you have a crystal ball, you have no way to predict how a fund will perform, except to look at the security's underlying risk. If a fund has existed long enough to build a track record through ups and downs, you can review its performance during the last stressful market.

Fortunately for all investors, some companies use a statistical measure called *standard deviation,* which measures the volatility in the fund's performance. The larger the swings in a fund's returns, the more likely the fund will slip into negative numbers.

Periodicals that report on and rank mutual funds include *All-Canadian Mutual Fund Guide* and *Canadian Mutual Fund Advisor,* available on newsstands or at your library.

Considering different types of mutual funds

As you prepare to invest in mutual funds, you need to decide which type of funds best suit your goals and tastes. Basically, you have the following four types of mutual funds to consider:

■ Equity funds, which invest in stocks

■ Bond funds (also considered income funds), which invest in bonds

■ Balanced funds, also called hybrid funds, which invest in both stocks and bonds

■ Money market funds, which hold short-term investments

Table 3-2 gives you a sense of how many dollars investors allocated to different types of mutual funds in 1998 and the change in those numbers in just one year to 1999.

Table 3-2:   Mutual Fund Assets in October 1998 and October 1999

Fund Type	Total Net Assets July 1998	Net Assets July 1999
Canadian Equity funds	$79.8 billion	$8.1 billion

Fund Type	Total Net Assets July 1998	Net Assets July 1999
Bond and Income funds	$28.9 billion	$31.4 billion
Balanced funds	$52.5 billion	$58.9 billion
Canadian Money Market funds	$33.5 billion	$43.2 billion

Source: The Investment Funds Institute of Canada

Each of these groups presents a wide variety of funds with different characteristics from which to choose. To help you further refine your search to match fund investments to your goals, the following lists offer a general look at some different types of funds available.

Equity funds include:

■ **Aggressive growth funds:** Managers of these funds are forever on the lookout for undiscovered, unheralded companies, including small and undervalued companies. The goal is to get in when the stock is cheap and realize substantial gains as it soars skyward. That dream doesn't always come true. But if you're willing to accept above-average risk, you may reap above-average gains.

■ **Growth funds:** These funds are among the mainstays of long-term investing. They own stocks in mostly large- or medium-sized companies whose significant earnings are expected to increase at a faster rate than that of the rest of the market. These growth funds do not typically pay dividends. Several types are available, including large-, medium-, and small-company growth funds.

■ **Value funds:** Managers of these funds seek out stocks that are underpriced — selling cheaply, relative to the stock's true value. The fund's manager believes that the market will recognize the stock's true price in the future. Stock price appreciation is long term. These funds don't typically turn in outstanding performance when the stock market is zooming along, but tend to hold their value a good deal more than growth funds when stock prices slide. That's why value funds are generally believed to be good hedges to more growth-oriented mutual funds. These funds come in large-, medium-, and small-company versions.

■ **Equity income funds:** These funds were developed to balance investors' desires for current income with some potential for capital appreciation. These fund managers invest mostly in stocks — often blue chip stocks — that pay dividends. They usually make some investments in utility companies, which are also likely to pay dividends.

■ **Growth and income funds:** These funds seek both capital appreciation and current income. Growth and income are considered equal investment objectives.

■ **International and global funds:** These two funds may sound like the same type of mutual fund, but they're not. *International funds* invest in a portfolio of stocks (international securities) outside of North America. *Global funds,* also called *world funds,* can invest anywhere in the world, including Canadian stock markets.

■ **Sector funds:** The managers of these funds concentrate their investments in one sector of the economy, such as financial services, real estate, technology, or precious metals. Although these types of funds may be a good choice after you've already built a portfolio that matches your investment plan, they have greater risk than almost any other type of fund because these funds concentrate their investments in one sector or industry.

Warning

If you're uncomfortable with the potential for significant losses, make sure that a sector fund only accounts for a small percentage of your portfolio — say, less than 10%. Remember, however, that if you invest in a balanced portfolio, your other investments should hold their own if only one industry is impacted.

- **Emerging market funds:** The managers of these funds seek out the stocks of underdeveloped economies, such as Asia, Eastern Europe, and Latin America. Finding undiscovered winners can prove advantageous, but an emerging market fund — also known as an emerging country fund — isn't a recommended mainstay for new investors because of the potential for loss. When these countries and economies suffer economic decline, they can create significant investor losses.

- **Region-specific or country-specific funds:** As their name implies, the managers of these funds look for the stock winners of one specific region or country of the world. Unless you have close relatives running a country somewhere and have firsthand knowledge about that land's economic prospects, you're wise to steer clear of these funds. The reason is simple: They have unmitigated risk from concentration in one area. For example, when Japan's economy declined in 1998, it sent mutual funds that invested exclusively in that country's companies tumbling by more than 50%.

- **Index funds:** The managers of these funds invest in stocks that mirror the investments tracked by an index such as the TSE 300 Composite Index. Some of the advantages of investing in index funds include low operating expenses, diversification, and potential tax savings. Although they don't necessarily rely on the performance of any one company or industry to buoy their performance, they do invest in equities that represent a market — such as the Toronto Stock Exchange. If and when that market dips, as the TSE did by more than 11% in 1987, index funds can be hit pretty hard.

Bond funds are less risky than stock funds, but also potentially less rewarding. You can choose from the following types of bond funds:

- Government of Canada bonds
- Provincial bonds
- Corporate bonds
- Chartered Bank bonds
- International bond funds

Balanced funds are another investment option. These funds are a mix of stocks and bonds that are also called *blended* or *hybrid funds.* Generally, managers invest in about 60% stocks and 40% bonds. Balanced funds are appealing to investors because even in bear markets, their bond holdings still allow them to pay dividends. (A *bear market* is generally defined as a market in which stock prices drop 20% or more from their previous high.)

Money market funds are, arguably, the least volatile type of mutual fund. Fund managers invest in instruments such as short-term bank GICs, Government of Canada Treasury bills, and short-term corporate debt issued by established and stable companies. This type of mutual fund is ideal for people who may need to use the money to buy something in the short term like a down payment on a home. These funds are also a convenient place to pool money for future investment decisions.

Analyzing mutual funds

As you begin your search for mutual funds, make sure that your performance evaluation produces meaningful results. Performance is important because good, long-term earnings enable you to maximize your investments and ensure that your money is working for you. Gauging future performance is not an exact science.

When you evaluate funds, check out periodicals like *Canadian Mutual Fund Advisor, All-Canadian Mutual Fund Guide, Gordon Pape's Mutual Funds Update,* and *Investor's Digest of Canada,* available by subscription, on newsstands, or at the library. A fund's prospectus, which you can request from a fund's toll-free phone number, also outlines the important features and objectives of the fund.

As an additional check on your selection process, compare all your choice funds before making a final decision; avoid choosing one fund in isolation. A single fund can look spectacular until you discover it trails most of its peers by 10%.

Look for the following information when you select mutual funds:

- **One-, three-, and five-year returns:** These numbers offer information on the fund's past performance. A look at all three can give you a sense of how well a fund fared over time and in relation to similar funds.

- **Year-to-date total returns:** This is a fund's report card for the current year, minus operating and management expenses. The numbers can give you a sense of whether earnings are in line with competing funds, out in front, or trailing.

Avoid the temptation to evaluate funds solely on returns to date. Past performance is no guarantee of future performance. Always look at the big picture, including the rest of the information on this list.

- **Maximum initial sales charges, commissions, or loads:** These are commissions you pay to a broker to buy a fund. A sales charge on a purchase, sometimes called a *load,* is a charge you pay when you buy shares. *No-load funds* don't charge sales loads. There are no-load funds in every major fund category. However, all mutual funds (whether load or no-load) have ongoing operating and management expenses.

In Canada, *front-end loads* (sales charges you pay to your brokerage at the time you purchase your mutual fund shares) are negotiable up to about 5%, but you'll find a lot in the 2% range. *Back-end loads* (also called *deferred sales charges* or *redemption fees,* paid when you sell your shares) are higher, in the 6-7% range. Typically, the longer you keep your shares, the lower the back-end load, with the charge going down about 1% every year.

- **Annual expenses:** Also called *management expense ratios (MERs),* these include both the fees paid to a fund's portfolio managers and a fund's expenses. The MER is always calculated as a percentage of the fund's total assets, and is paid out of those assets. Before you settle on one fund, review the numbers on at least a few competitors. In general, the more aggressive a fund, the more expenses it incurs trading investments. Before you invest in a particular fund, be cautious if it has an extremely high MER compared to that of similar funds. You can find out how a fund's MER has fluctuated over the past five years by reading its annual report.

To develop a sense of how expenses can take a big bite out of earnings over the years, consider this example: A $10,000 investment earns 10% over 40 years with a 1% expense ratio, which yields a return of $302,771. The same investment with a 1.74% expense ratio returns $239,177, or $63,594 less.

- **Manager's tenure:** Consider how long the current fund manager (or managers) has been managing the fund. If it's only been a year or two, take that into consideration before you invest — the five-year record that caught your eye may have been created by someone who has already moved down the road. Fund managers move around often. In an ideal world, your funds are handled by managers with staying power.

- **Portfolio turnover:** This tells you how often a fund manager sells stocks in the course of a year. Selling stocks is expensive, so high turnover over the long run will probably hurt performance. If two funds appear equal in all other aspects, but one has high turnover and the other low turnover, by all means choose the fund with low turnover.

- **Underlying fund investments:** For your own sake, take a look at the top five or ten stocks or bonds that a fund is investing in. For example, a growth fund may be getting its rapid appreciation from a high concentration in fairly risky technology stocks, or a global fund may have many of its holdings here in the Canadian stock market. Neither of these strategies is a mortal sin if you know about and can live with it. If you can't, keep looking for a fund that matches your goals. Looking at underlying investments not only helps minimize your surprises as markets and economies shift, but also enables you to create a balanced portfolio.

CHAPTER 4

UNDERSTANDING STOCKS, BONDS, AND BEYOND

IN THIS CHAPTER

- Discovering stocks
- Understanding bond basics
- Realizing the potential of real estate

The investments we describe in this chapter carry a great potential for return — but that possibility of return comes at a greater risk to your money. Stocks, bonds, and real estate are investment options whose value fluctuates with the market, meaning that the value of these investments can grow and shrink greatly. However, with the information we give you in this chapter, you will be able to make good educated guesses about how to pursue these investments.

Sizing Up Stocks

A *stock* is a piece of paper that signifies that you own part of a company. The market price of a stock is directly related to the profits and the losses of the company. In other words, when the company profits, the worth of your stock increases. When the company falters and its profits decline, so does the worth of your stock.

Investors who buy stock own shares of the company. That's why they're called *shareholders*.

Understanding how stocks work

Companies issue stock to raise money to fund a variety of initiatives, including expansion, the development of new products, the acquisition of other companies, or the paying off of debt. In an action called an *initial public offering (IPO),* a company opens sale of its stock to investors.

An investment banker helps underwrite the public stock offering. By *underwrite,* we mean that the investment banker helps the company determine when to go public and what price the stock should be at that time.

When the stock begins selling, the price can rise or fall from its set price depending on whether investors believe that the stock was fairly and accurately priced. Often, the price of an IPO soars during the first few days of trading, but then can later fall back to earth.

After the IPO, stock prices will continue to fluctuate, based on what investors are willing to accept when they buy or sell the stock. In simple terms, stock prices are a matter of supply and demand. If everyone wants a stock, its price rises, sometimes sharply. If, on the other hand, investors are fearful that, for example, the company's management is faltering and has taken on too much debt to sustain strong growth, they may begin selling in noticeable volume. Mass sales can drive the price down. In addition to specific company issues, the price can drop for other reasons, including bad news for the entire industry or a general downturn in the overall economy.

Stocks are bought and sold on stock exchanges, such as the Toronto Stock Exchange and the Vancouver Stock Exchange in Canada, as well as on exchanges around the world, like the New York Stock Exchange and the Tokyo Stock Exchange. Companies that don't have the cash reserves necessary to be listed on one of the exchanges are traded *over-the-counter,*

which means that they receive less scrutiny from analysts and large investors such as mutual fund managers.

In addition, professional analysts who are paid to watch companies and their stocks can give a thumbs-up or a thumbs-down to a stock, which in turn can send stock prices soaring or plummeting. These stock analysts sit in brokerage firms on New York's fabled Wall Street and Toronto's Bay Street. The analyst's job is to watch closely the actions of public companies and their managers and the results those actions produce.

By carefully monitoring news about a company's earnings, corporate strategies, new products and services, and legal and regulatory problems and victories, analysts give stocks a *buy, sell,* or *hold* rating. Such opinions can have a wide-sweeping impact on the price of a stock, at least in the short term. Rumblings, real or imagined, can send the price of a stock, or the stock market overall, tumbling downward or soaring skyward.

The price of stock goes up and down — a phenomenon known as *volatility* — but if the news creating the stir is short-term, panic is an overreaction. You don't want to sell a stock when its price is down, only to see it make a miraculous recovery a few days, weeks, or even months down the road.

Smart investors who have done their research and are invested for the longer term won't be impacted by short-term price dips or panics. Unless, of course, you use the opportunity to buy a stock you've already researched and were going to buy anyway. The old adage — buy low, sell high — holds as true today as it did 75 years ago.

How low can stock prices go? In October 1987, the much-watched Dow Jones Industrial Average (DJIA) tumbled by 22.6%. This decline meant that the value of a $10,000 investment dropped to $7,740. Many stocks recovered, but some did not. On Bay Street, the TSE 300 Composite Index lost 11.32% of its value.

You can lose all your money with a stock investment, and that risk is why you need to analyze your choices carefully. The three most basic types of risks associated with stock investments are:

■ You may lose money.

■ Your stocks may not perform as well as other, similar stocks.

■ A loss may threaten your financial goals.

Stock investing carries certain risks, but they can be minimized by careful investment selection and by diversification, a technique for building a balanced portfolio, which we investigate more thoroughly in Chapter 8.

Recognizing different types of stock

Companies issue two basic kinds of stock, *common* and *preferred,* and each provides shareholders with different opportunities and rights:

■ **Common stock:** Represents ownership in a company. Companies can pay what are called *dividends* to their shareholders. Dividends are paid out from a company's earnings and can fluctuate with the company's performance. *Note:* Not all companies pay dividends.

Common stock offers no performance guarantees, and although this kind of stock has historically outperformed other types of investments, you can lose your entire investment if a company does poorly enough to wipe out its earnings and reputation into the foreseeable future. Common stock dividends are paid only after the preferred stock dividends are paid.

■ **Preferred stock:** Constitutes ownership in shares as well, but this stock differs from common stock in ways that reduce risk to investors, but also limit *upside potential,* or upward trends in stock pricing. Dividends on preferred stock are paid before common stock, so preferred stock may be a better bet for investors who rely on the income from these payments. But the dividend, which is set, is not increased when the company profits, and the price of preferred stock increases more slowly than that of common stock. Also, preferred stock investors stand a better chance of getting their money back if the company declares bankruptcy.

A company's stock is also categorized depending on its perceived expected performance. Basically, a company's stock falls into one of two categories: *growth* or *value* (see Table 4-1 for a summary of each).

Table 4-1: The Differences between Growth Stocks and Value Stocks

Investor Characteristics	Pros	Cons
Growth Stocks	Investors anticipate higher profits in return for higher stock prices. The return on investment can be substantial and prove worth the risk	They are less likely to pay dividends; and if they do, they're typically lower than that of value stocks. Stock prices tend to be affected by negative company news and short-term market changes.
Value Stocks	Investors anticipate that the company will experience a turnaround that will produce higher profits in the future. It costs fewer investment dollars to buy a dollar of their profits.	They may never realize the potential that investors project onto them.

Over time, you're likely to buy a mix of both types of stocks for your portfolio, so knowing the different characteristics of each is important. Understanding growth and value stocks can help you evaluate your options more carefully.

Growth companies are typically organizations with a positive outlook for expansion and, ultimately, stock prices that move upward. Investors looking for growth companies usually are willing to pay a higher price for stocks that have consistently produced higher profits because they're betting the companies will continue to perform well in the future.

Because they use their money to invest in future growth, growth companies are less likely to pay dividends than other, more conservative companies; when they do pay dividends, the amounts tend to be lower. An investor who buys a growth stock believes that, according to analysis of the company's history and statistics, the company is likely to continue to produce strong earnings and is therefore worth its higher price.

The stock of a growth company is, however, somewhat riskier because the price tends to react to negative company news and short-term changes in the market. Also, the company may not continue to produce earnings that are worth its higher price.

In contrast, value stocks are out of favour, left on the shelf by investors who are busy reaching for more expensive and trendier items. For that reason, you spend fewer dollars to buy a dollar of their profits than if you invest in a growth stock. When investors buy value stocks, they're betting that they're actually buying a turnaround story — with a happy ending down the road.

Value companies carry risk too, because they may never reach what investors believe is their true potential. Optimism doesn't always pay off in profits.

Identifying potential stock investments

What do you need to know to determine which stocks are potential investments? To get started, stick with stocks relating to your own interests or knowledge. If you frequent particular stores or restaurants and you use and like their products and services, find out if they are publicly held companies. Start identifying and watching these stocks. That advice doesn't mean that you should buy their stock right away. You still have some homework to do.

The following list tells you what to look for when investigating potential stock investments. Investment periodicals like *The Investment Reporter, Investor's Digest of Canada, Financial Post Investment Reports* and *Blue Book of Stock Reports,* along with the U.S. publication *ValueLine* (www.valueline.com) and any brokerage firm analyst report can provide you with much or all of the following pertinent facts and measures (see Chapter 7 for more information on working with brokerages):

■ **Find out if the industry is growing.** Some industries aren't. News stories on the industry in question can tell you the state of the industry (also check out *The Globe and Mail Report on Business, National Post Financial Post* or *Canadian Business* magazine). The company's annual report can also be a useful source for this kind of information.

Company shareholder departments can provide you with copies of annual reports and quarterly reports that companies must file. You can also find them at major public libraries, or on the Internet at www.sedar.com. Keep in mind that once you buy a stock, thereby becoming a shareholder, the company will be required by law to send you a copy of its annual reports.

■ **Find primary competitors.** Don't look at a stock in isolation. A company that looks enticing by itself may look like a 100-pound weakling when you evaluate its strengths and weaknesses next to the leading competitors in the industry. Check out at least two competitors of any stock you're evaluating.

- **Check out annual earnings and sales.** This is key in deciphering how quickly a company is growing over one-year, three-year, and five-year time periods, and whether its earnings are keeping pace with sales. Look for growth rates of at least 10%.

- **Look at the stock's price-to-earnings (P/E) ratios.** This is the primary means of evaluating a stock. The *P/E ratio* is derived by dividing a stock's share price by its earnings-per-share. The result tells you how much investors are willing to pay for each $1 of earnings. Those stocks that have faster earnings growth rates also tend to carry higher P/Es, which means that investors are willing to pay through the nose to own shares. The value of a P/E ratio, however, can be subjective. One investor may think that a particular company's P/E ratio of 20 is high, while another may consider it low to moderate.

- **Find out the price-to-book value (P/B) ratio.** The *P/B ratio* is the stock's share price divided by *book value,* or a firm's assets minus its liabilities. This ratio is a good comparison tool and can tell you which companies are asset-rich and which are carrying more debt.

A low P/B ratio can be an indicator that a stock may be a good value investment.

- **Check out the stock's price-to-growth flow ratio.** This ratio is the share price divided by *growth flow* (annual earnings plus research and development costs) per share. This is a useful measure for assessing fast-moving companies, especially in the technology sector, where management often puts profits back into product development.

- **Look at the stock's PEG ratio.** The *PEG ratio* is a company's P/E ratio divided by its expected earnings' growth rate and is an indicator of well-priced stock.

- **Look ahead.** Projections of five-year annual growth rates and five-year P/E ratios can tell you whether analysts believe that the companies you're evaluating can continue to grow at their current rate, can beat it, or will start to fall behind.

Make a list of the stocks you are interested in and watch their performance over time. Doing so gives you a feel for how the stocks respond to different types of economic and market news. You can also see which stocks' prices move around and are more volatile.

So, does your own analysis indicate that you have a winner on your hands or a dog? If you're unsure, sit tight and watch what happens in the weeks and months ahead. Watching several stocks over a period of time not only tells you how well they're doing, or not doing, it can also show you how well you're honing your own stock analysis skills.

Chapter 7 tells you how to purchase a stock after doing your research.

Learning about Bond Basics

A bond is basically an IOU. When you purchase a bond, you are lending money to a government, municipality, corporation, federal agency, or other entity. In return for the loan, the entity promises to pay you a specified rate of interest during the life of the bond and to repay the *face value* (the *principal*) of the bond when it matures (or comes due).

When you buy a new bond from the original *issuer* (the entity to whom you're lending your money), you will purchase it at face value, also called *par value*, and you will be promised a specific rate of interest, called the *coupon*. If you buy a bond that's already been resold before maturity (from what's called the *secondary market*, where existing bonds are bought and sold), you may buy it at a *discount* (less than par) or at a *premium* (above par).

Bonds aren't like stocks. You are not buying part ownership in a company or government when you purchase a bond. Instead, what you're actually buying — or betting on — is the issuer's ability to pay you back with interest.

Understanding how bonds work

You have a number of important variables to consider when you invest in bonds, including the stability of the issuer, the bond's maturity or due date, interest rate, price, yield, tax status, and risk. As with any investment, ensuring that all these variables match up with your own investment goals is key to making the right choice for your money.

Be sure to buy a bond with a maturity date that tracks with your financial plans. For instance, if you have a child's post-secondary education to fund 15 years from now and you want to invest part of his or her education fund in bonds, you need to select vehicles that have maturities that match that need. If you have to sell a bond before its due date, you receive the prevailing market price, which may be more or less than the price you paid.

In general, because they often specify the yield you'll be paid, bonds can't make you a millionaire overnight like a stock can. What can you expect to earn? That depends on a number of factors, including the type of bond you buy, and market conditions, like prevailing interest rates. What can you expect to lose? That depends on how safe the issuer is. Read more about this issue in Chapter 5.

Recognizing different types of bonds

Bonds come in all shapes and sizes, and they enable you to choose one that meets your needs in terms of your investment time horizon, risk profile, and income needs. First, here is a look at the different types of Government of Canada securities available:

■ **Treasury bills:** T-Bills are offered in 3-month, 6-month, and 12-month maturities. These short-term government securities do not pay current interest, but instead are always sold at a discount price, which is lower than par value. The difference between the discount price and the par value received is considered interest (and is taxed as income). For example, if you pay the discount price of $950 for a $1,000 T-bill, you pay 5% less than you actually get back when the bill matures. Par is considered to be $100 worth of a bond (which, although selling for a $1,000 minimum, is always expressed in a $100 measure for the purpose of valuation). The minimum investment for T-bills is $5,000, but you can subsequently purchase them in $1,000 increments.

■ **Government of Canada bonds:** Unlike T-bills, Government of Canada bonds have fixed coupons that pay a specific interest at regular intervals (every six months). These bonds are longer-term offerings than T-bills, with maturities of between 1 and 30 years. Typically, the longer the term, the higher the interest paid. The minimum investment is lower than for T-bills, just $1,000. But they are also issued in larger denominations. The interest you earn on Government of Canada bonds is considered income and taxed as such. If the face value of your bond accrues, this is considered a capital gain.

■ **Strip or Zero-coupon bonds:** Strip bonds, so named because the coupon has been "stripped" from the bond's principal, work almost like T-bills. They are sold at a steep discount, and interest accrues (builds up) during the life of the bond. At maturity, the investor receives all the accrued interest plus the original investment. Strip bonds are guaranteed by the federal government, and can be sold anytime. As with T-bills, the difference between the discounted price you pay for a strip bond and the value at maturity is considered income, and is fully taxed.

■ **Canada Savings Bonds (CSBs):** These have long been a fall investment ritual for Canadians. You purchase Canada Savings Bonds from your bank, trust, credit union, or investment dealer during the annual selling season. For 1999, that season lasts between October 4, 1999 and April 1, 2000. The bond is registered to you and is non-transferable. The value of the bond itself never changes, so these bonds are not tradeable.

Quite simply, by buying a Canada Savings Bond, you are lending your money to the federal government in return for interest. With a regular-interest CBS, that gain is paid out once a year, on November 1, and is taxable as income. With compound-interest CSBs, your interest is reinvested until maturity, thereby compounding your gains, but, as of 1990, you still have to claim it as income each year. For more zest, the government also offers an indexed CSB, which takes into account rising interest rates. The bond's yield is based on the inflation rate plus a fixed rate of return. For more information on CSBs, visit the federal government's Canada Investment and Savings Web site at www.cis-pec.gc.ca.

While Government of Canada bonds are some of the safest investment bets around — since they're guaranteed by the strength of the federal government — remember that risk and reward are tradeoffs that you need to look at in tandem. As with all investments, the safer the investment the less you're likely to earn or lose!

The following are other types of available bonds:

- **Provincial bonds:** Provincial governments issue both T-bills and bonds (short-, medium- and long-term), much like the federal government. While these are safe investments, bonds issued by provinces facing economic uncertainty, like Quebec or Newfoundland, are considered slightly more risky by investors. In return for the added risk, they usually pay a higher yield.

- **Municipal bonds:** These are loans you make to a local government, whether it's in your city or town.

- **Commercial paper:** These are short-term debt instruments employed by both publicly owned Crown corporations (referred to as Government Guaranteed Commercial Paper) and private sector corporations. Like T-bills and strip bonds, they are sold at a discount, but yields tend to be higher.

- **Corporate bonds:** A growing area in Canada, these are issued by companies that need to raise money, including public utilities and transportation companies, industrial corporations and manufacturers, and financial service companies.

Corporate bonds can be riskier than either Canadian government bonds or provincial bonds because companies can go bankrupt. So a company's credit risk is an important tool for evaluating the safety of a corporate bond. Even if an organization doesn't throw in the towel, its risk factor can be enough to cause agency analysts to downgrade the company's overall rating. If that happens, you may find it more difficult to sell the bond early.

- **Junk bonds:** Junk bonds pay high yields because the issuer may be in financial trouble, have a poor credit rating, and are likely to have a difficult time finding buyers for their issues. Although you may decide that junk bonds or junk bond mutual funds have a place in your portfolio, make sure that spot is small because these bonds carry high risk.

Although junk bonds may look particularly attractive at times, think twice before you buy. They don't call them junk for nothing. You could potentially suffer a total loss if the issuer declares bankruptcy. As one wag suggested, if you really believe in the company so much, invest in its stock, which has unlimited upside potential.

Identifying potential bond investments

Here's a look at some items you need to evaluate before investing in a fund:

- **Issuer stability:** This is also known as *credit quality,* which assesses an issuer's ability to pay back its debts, including the interest and principal it owes its bond holders, in full and on time. Although many corporations, the Canadian government and the provinces have never defaulted on a bond, you can expect that some issuers can and will be unable to repay. (Chapter 5 tells you more about assessing issuer stability.)

- **Maturity:** A bond's maturity refers to the specific future date when you can expect your principal to be repaid. Bond maturities can range from as short as one day all the way up to 30 years. Make sure that the bond you select has a maturity date that works with your needs. T-bills and strip bonds pay interest at maturity. All other bonds pay interest twice yearly or quarterly. Most investors buy bonds in order to have a steady flow of income (from interest).

    The longer the maturity in a bond, the more risk associated with it — that is, the greater the fluctuation in bond value based upon changes in interest rates.

- **Interest rate:** Bonds pay interest that can be fixed-rate, floating, or payable at maturity. Most bond rates are fixed until maturity, and the amount is based on a percentage of the face or principal amount.

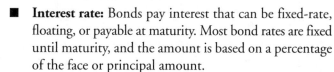

■ **Face value:** This is the stated value of a bond. The bond is selling at a *premium* when the price is above its face value; pricing below its face value means that it's selling at a *discount*.

■ **Price:** The price you pay for a bond is based on an array of different factors, including current interest rates, supply and demand, and maturity.

■ **Current yield:** This is the annual percentage rate of return earned on a bond. You can find a bond's current yield by dividing the bond's interest payment by its purchase price. For example, if you bought a bond at $900 and its interest rate is 8% (0.08), the current yield is 8.89% — 8% or 0.08 ÷ $900 = 8.89.

■ **Yield to maturity (YTM):** This tells you the total return you can expect to receive if you hold a bond until it matures. Its calculation takes into account the bond's face value, its current price, and the years left until the bond matures. The calculation is an elaborate one, but the broker you're buying a bond from should be able to give you its YTM. The YTM also enables you to compare bonds with different maturities and yields.

Don't buy a bond on current yield alone. Ask the bank or brokerage firm from whom you're buying the bond to provide a YTM figure so that you can have a clear idea about the bond's real value to your portfolio.

■ **Tax status:** Outside your RRSP, the interest you earn on bonds is fully taxable as income. The difference between what you paid for a discounted bond and the value at maturity is also considered income. Gains you make on the value of a bond if you sell it before maturity are considered a capital gain. You will be taxed on 75% of your capital gains annually.

If you sell a Government of Canada, provincial, municipal, or corporate bond for more than you paid for it, you'll pay tax on the difference, which is considered a capital gain.

Revenue Canada will tax you on 75% of that gain. Turn to Chapter 7 to find out how to purchase a bond, if you are so inclined.

Investing in Real Estate

There are three ways that you can become a real estate investor: first, by buying your own home; second, by buying an investment property; and third, by investing in a real estate investment trust (REIT).

Although it's true that over time, real estate owners and investors have enjoyed rates of return comparable to the stock market, real estate is not a simple way to get wealthy. Nor is it for the faint of heart or the passive investor. Real estate goes through good and bad performance periods, and most people who make money in real estate do so because they invest over many years.

Buying your own home

Most people invest in real estate by becoming homeowners. Canadians have long been taught that the *equity*, which is the difference between the market value of your home and the loan owed on it, increases over time to produce a significant part of your net worth.

Unless you have the good fortune to live in a rent-controlled apartment, owning a home should be less expensive than renting a comparable home throughout your adult life. Why? As a renter, your housing costs will follow the level of inflation, while as a homeowner, the bulk of your housing costs are not exposed to inflation if you have a fixed-rate mortgage.

Figure 4-1 illustrates the difference in expenditure when comparing owning and renting a home. In this graph, we assume that the homeowner has a 30-year, fixed-rate mortgage of

Figure 4-1: The expense of owning versus renting your home.

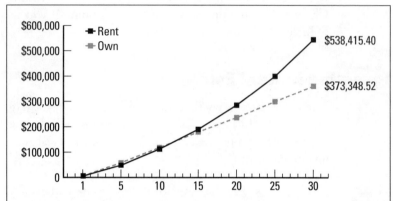

7.5% on $150,000, and the renter starts out with an $800 per month rent payment with annual increases of 4%.

Figure 4-1 shows that at the end of 30 years the renter has paid over $500,000, while the owner has paid less than $375,000. What's more, the owner has increased her equity, also called *net worth*. Owning your home can add to your sense of financial security as the economy fluctuates. In addition to the financial benefits, home ownership gives you more control over your own living space; for example, it allows you more freedom to decorate your home's exterior and interior according to your own tastes. And the federal government gives homeowners another major financial boost. How? Any profit made when you sell your primary residence is tax-free. This is called the *principal residence exemption* and each Canadian family is entitled to one.

Buying an investment property

A second way to invest in real estate is to buy residential housing such as single-family homes or multi-unit buildings, and rent them. In many ways, buying real estate in this way isn't an investment; it's a business. Maintaining a property can easily turn into a part-time job. If you're a person who dreams of putting heart and soul into a property, however, it may be worth investigating. If you do decide to take this route, first, be sure that you have sufficient time to devote to the project. Second, be careful not to sacrifice contributions to your RRSP in order to own investment real estate.

Remember

Deciding to become a real estate investor depends mostly on you and your situation. Ask yourself the following questions: Is real estate something that you have an affinity for? Do you know a lot about houses, or have a knack for spotting up-and-coming areas? Are you cut out to handle the responsibilities that come with being a landlord? Do you have the time to manage your property?

Another drawback to real estate investment is that you earn no tax benefits while you're accumulating your down payment, whereas your RRSP gives you an immediate tax deduction as you contribute money to it. If you haven't exhausted your contributions to your RRSP, consider doing so before taking a look at investment real estate.

Investing in a real estate investment trust (REIT)

Publicly traded REITs are new to Canada. REITs are real estate investment companies that purchase and manage rental real estate for investors. Some REITs may be specialized in one particular type of property, while others invest in different types of property, such as shopping centres, apartments, and other rental buildings. You can invest in REITs either through purchasing them directly on a major stock exchange like the TSE or through a real estate mutual fund that invests in numerous REITs.

CHAPTER 5

MAKING GOOD FIRST STEPS IN THE MARKET

IN THIS CHAPTER

- Starting out with mutual fund investing
- Beginning to invest in the stock market
- Exploring possibilities in the bond market

Everyone wants a great portfolio of investments, but where do you start? Like any other journey, you begin with that unceremonious first step. If you make the move, you can be on your way to financial comfort and freedom. Sit around for a few more years thinking about what you should be doing, and you'll be that much further behind.

Of course, picking your first investment is not something to do rashly. View your investments as long-term commitments. Don't impulsively make a purchase, thinking that you can change your mind later. Many financial experts recommend a simple approach: Buy one bond fund, one international stock mutual fund, one money market fund, and one Canadian equity mutual fund. And then have confidence in your decision.

First Steps in Mutual Fund Investing

Mutual funds can be a great fit for a first-time investor. Because a professional manages them, you don't have to wrack your brain about what individual stock or bond to buy or when to buy or sell it. At the same time, you get a fairly diversified portfolio in one fell swoop, which involves much less risk than if you invest in only one stock.

Figure 5-1 shows just how popular mutual funds have become with Canadian investors.

Figure 5-1: Mutual funds have become a favourite with Canadian investors

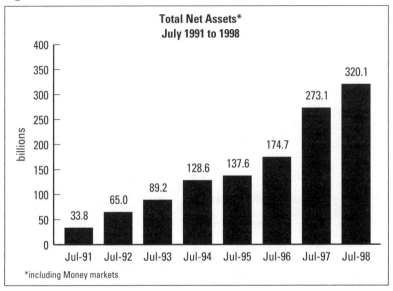

Total Net Assets*
July 1991 to 1998

*including Money markets

Source: The Investment Funds Institute of Canada

If you're uncomfortable with the kind of risk that stocks present, find a good mutual fund for your launch into investing. Starting out with a mutual fund doesn't represent the end of your quest; it's the beginning. You can always select a handful of decent stocks down the road to add to your portfolio.

According to the Investment Funds Institute of Canada, there are now more than 2,000 mutual funds to choose from in Canada. With that kind of choice, the world may be your oyster, but you eventually have to make selections that suit you best. In the next three sections, we talk about three types of mutual funds that can be good first investments.

Make sure that you check out one-, three-, five- and ten-year performance track records for a fund you are considering. This kind of research can yield valuable information. You want to see consistent returns over time and relatively low expenses (ideally 2% or less). It can also give you a sense of how a manager approaches his or her investments, and whether the style is more aggressive than you are comfortable dealing with. (See Chapter 3 for more tips on what to look for as you shop for mutual funds.)

Also review the fund's prospectus, which outlines its investment objectives and policies, expenses, and risks. Some better mutual fund companies are starting to graphically depict the worst quarter and year they've experienced, along with the best, so that you can quickly get an idea of how low and high the fund may go with your money.

Balanced funds

Although managers of balanced funds invest to earn respectable returns, they manage first and foremost to avoid sizable losses. To do this, many invest in bonds. In some fund portfolios, bonds account for 30% or more of the balanced fund's holdings.

Balanced funds seek income and capital preservation as their goal, so they offer moderate capital appreciation as compared to growth funds. Balanced funds don't take as hard a hit as more aggressive funds when the market dips.

Large Canadian growth funds

Large Canadian growth fund managers look for large and mid-size Canadian companies that are fairly stable performers, but have the potential to continue growing. Changes in society, such as the aging of the baby boom generation, may be one reason that some companies have good growth potential. For example, some managers like companies in health care, entertainment, travel, and financial services because they have the potential to benefit from the dollars of older, richer boomers.

A large-company growth index fund

A manager of an index fund invests in companies whose stocks are listed in an index such as the TSE 300 Composite Index. The fund tracks the performance of the index. The TSE 300 is the best-recognized Canadian stock market index. (See Chapter 8 for details on the TSE 300 and other indices.)

Rather than trying to predict the direction of the market, index funds are designed to match the performance of the index. These funds are considered to be unmanaged because they invest and hold the same stocks as in the index.

Unfortunately, the fact that index funds match the performance of the index is the worst part, too, because in a bear market (when stock prices drop significantly), index funds have no place else to turn for investments but to the index. Remember, however, that index funds can offer the investor long-term, steady growth.

You can pick a small-company mutual fund, a medium-company mutual fund, a bond mutual fund, and an international mutual fund as you continue building your portfolio, but it's a good idea to start with a fund that invests in large-company stocks. Because, since the late 1920s, these types of stock have historical average annual returns of about 11%, this type of fund can anchor the rest of your portfolio.

Table 5-1 shows a concise view of the characteristics that differentiate these three types of mutual funds.

Table 5-1:   Mutual Fund Characteristics

Balanced funds	Most conservative of the stock mutual funds. Fund managers are first and foremost concerned with avoiding big losses; then they concentrate on getting respectable returns.

continued

Table 5-1: Mutual Fund Characteristics (continued)

Large Canadian growth funds	Fund managers invest in large and mid-size Canadian companies that have shown stable returns but have the potential to continue growing.
Large-company growth index funds	Returns match the index's performance and don't rely on the picks of fund managers.

Do you think that you need a fortune to get started in mutual fund investing? You're wrong. Many fund companies will let you start with as little as $25-50, if you're willing to continue contributing monthly.

First Steps in Stock Investing

If you're willing to roll up your sleeves and do the research necessary to invest in individual companies, a stock may be a good fit for your new portfolio. The key is to avoid excessive risk. The best way to minimize risk is to buy a solid company — one that is essentially a blue chip or a larger-company growth stock. Look for a stock with consistent performance that appears to sustain and even increase over time.

The TSE 35 is the Canadian index of blue chips, listing the likes of Inco, Seagram, Imperial Oil, and Canadian Pacific. (See Chapter 8 for details about the TSE 35.) These stocks tend to hedge investors' first exposure to equity investing by paying dividends that offset any lacklustre performance.

You may also want to seek out a *value stock* — a stock that has been underperforming its peers, but that seems poised to turn things around. In the U.S., there's even an index called "Dogs of the Dow," which is compiled by Dow Jones and printed in *The Wall Street Journal,* listing specifically those stocks that are on the outs. Of course, none is guaranteed to become the next best stock to own. You have to judge for yourself by looking at a company's long-term growth and earnings; its price-to-earnings (P/E) ratio; and any company news that can give you insight into debt level, acquisitions on the horizon, and competitive edge of products, services, and management. (The P/E ratio is derived by dividing a stock's share price by its earnings-per-share price. The result shows how much investors are willing to pay for each $1 of earnings — see Chapter 4 for details.)

Annual reports, which you can request from a company's own investor relations department, can give you some of these details. For the rest, you have to sift through analysts' reports and check the charts that are available from Canadian publications like *Investor's Digest of Canada, The MoneyLetter, The Investment Reporter, Financial Post Investment Reports,* or *Blue Book of Stock Reports.* These subscription services can show you a stock's ups and downs over the years and even over the past month. Analysts' reports can project a company's earnings, dividends, and price growth over the next few months and years.

Don't forget to check on competitors, too. Because all performance data is relative, a company that may seem like a great catch may actually be inferior to its peers, but you won't know that if you don't check. For example, if you're thinking about investing in McDonald's, make sure that you check out the stocks for Tim Horton's, too.

First Steps in Bond Investing

If you're in or near retirement and consider safety, or reduced risk, a priority, you can buy a bond. There is a minimum investment for Government of Canada bonds of $1,000, and they are traded in $1,000 increments. Before you buy a bond, determine how long you want to hold the bond, which tells you what maturity date you're after; how safe the bond you want to own must be; and how much interest (yield) you need.

Short-term Government of Canada bonds are the safest, but highly rated provincial bonds and corporate bonds can be almost as safe. To determine if the extra risk is warranted, compare the rates paid by the bonds you're considering with the rates paid by Government of Canada Treasury bills. Because T-bills are the safest investment, if other bonds aren't paying much more, there may be little reason to take on the additional risk.

If you're not sure, comparison-shop. If a bond isn't issued by the Canadian government, check the issuer's financial position by its quality rating with a bond rating service like Canadian Bond Rating Service (CBRS) or Dominion Bond Rating Service (DBRS). Table 5-2 shows the rating system used by the CBRS for long-term bonds. Stick with a bond with a rating of A or above. (See Chapter 4 for more about bonds.)

Table 5-2: Canadian Bond Rating Service Credit Ratings

Highest quality	A++
Very good quality	A+
Good quality	A
Medium quality	B++
Lower quality	B+
Poor quality	B
Speculative quality	C
Default	D
Rating suspended	Suspended

Can a bond issuer meet its bond and other debt obligations on time, in full? That's the question that is analyzed closely by rating agencies such as Canadian Bond Rating Service and Dominion Bond Rating Service. Before buying a bond, checking a bond's rating should become a routine part of any purchase. Ask the broker or bank you're buying from to see the rating.

The consensus, especially for beginning investors, is to steer clear of anything not rated A or above by the CBRS or DBRS.

Be sure to find out how low the bonds or underlying bond investments have dipped in terms of performance over the years. You can then gauge your own exposure, although if you hold a bond until maturity, the mountains and valleys of performance don't matter.

If you're buying a government bond or bond fund, you may also want to consider whether you want the investment inside your RRSP or outside. Remember, interest-bearing investments like Government of Canada bonds are fully taxed annually outside your RRSP. Inside, those gains are sheltered from tax.

The Don'ts of First-Time Investing in Mutual Funds, Stocks, and Bonds

No one wants you to become so overwhelmed by the prospect of the seemingly endless investment choices that you hesitate to start. At the same time, before you get carried away, here are a few wise words that may help protect you as you set out to achieve your investment goals.

Don't invest for the short-term

Plan to invest only what you can afford to tuck away for years. Even if the stock market crashes the day after you buy your first investment, you stand a much better chance of recovering your dollars if you have five or more years to stay invested, instead of having to cash in investments next month or next year.

Don't play with fire

Avoid speculative, risky investments, especially those whose terms and properties you can't understand no matter how many times a broker or friend explains them. Your comfort level is important, so remember that some of the best investment options can seem boring and mundane.

Risky investments include those based on premises that seem far-fetched, such as an underwater casino, or those that promise unbelievable returns. They may also have terms that are unfavourable, such as an investment that gives a company or other investors the right to buy you out at the price you paid if the investment turns profitable.

If an investment seems too good to be true, it is.

Don't put all your eggs in one basket

Just because one type of investment is doing well this month or this year doesn't mean that its success will continue or that you should invest all your money in that arena. Also, you don't want to scare yourself out of continued investing by choosing a highly volatile investment that may start losing your dollars immediately.

Don't forget to do your homework

Wise investing relies on research, which can be hard work. Just because someone touts an investment in an Internet chat room or across the lunch table at work doesn't mean it's a good buy. Do your homework. If you wouldn't buy an investment except for the go-go advice, don't buy it.

CHAPTER 6

TAKING THE PLUNGE INTO SELF-SERVE INVESTMENTS

IN THIS CHAPTER

- Shopping for savings accounts and tiered accounts
- Knowing what to ask about GICs

We talk about the basics of self-serve investments — including savings accounts, and GICs — in Chapter 2. When it's time to roll up your sleeves and actually get your money invested in these vehicles, this chapter tells you how to take the plunge.

Diving into Savings Accounts

Rather than "taking the plunge," opening a savings account is more like dipping your toe into the water. But we've all got to start somewhere, and this is where many people start out. Opening a savings account can be the first step to a lifetime of good savings habits.

You've probably heard the advice "Pay yourself first." That doesn't mean give yourself some cash so that you can go shopping. When you sit down to pay bills, write the first cheque to a savings or investment account. It doesn't matter if you start with a very small amount, just make savings a habit. And when you get bonuses and raises, you can increase those cheques you write to yourself.

When you shop for a bank, credit union, or trust where you can open a savings account, make sure to ask the following questions:

- **Is there a required minimum balance for a savings account?** Some institutions charge a fee if your balance falls below a required minimum.

- **What are your fees for savings accounts?** You can expect to be charged either a monthly or quarterly maintenance fee. The institution may also charge you a fee if you close the account before a specified period of time.

- **How much interest will I get on my savings?** Expect less than 1% interest.

- **Is the account federally insured?** Ask specifically whether the institution has Canada Deposit Insurance Corporation (CDIC) insurance. If it does, then you can get up to $60,000 of your savings back if the bank fails.

- **What services do you offer?** Many banks now offer banking by telephone or the Internet.

- **Does the bank use a tiered account system?** A tiered account system allows you to earn higher interest if your account balance is consistently over an amount specified by the bank.

- **Does the bank pay higher interest on the entire balance in a tiered account?** Some banks only pay you the higher rate on the amount above the minimum needed to receive that rate.

Call around to at least three different institutions — banks, trusts, and/or credit unions — to compare their offerings. You can also call brokerage firms, which offer GICs, to find out their minimums and fees.

If the answers to all of these questions come out about equal, choose the institution that's most convenient for you and offers the best service, convenient hours, friendly tellers — whatever suits your banking habits best. Savings accounts come in several types, including:

- **The basic savings account:** These usually require a minimum opening deposit of $100.

- **The tiered savings account:** These often require a higher minimum opening balance and pay a higher yield than basic accounts. For example, you might earn 1% interest with a $5,000 account balance, but as much as 3% interest or more with a balance of 60,000. The downside to tiered accounts is that some pay no interest at all on balances below the imposed minimum. Be sure to ask before you invest in this type of account.

- **The package deal:** These new-age savings accounts may permit extra privileges, like cheque-writing.

When you're in front of your friendly neighbourhood bank representative, ask the questions contained in the worksheet in Table 6-1. Shop around to at least three different institutions before you commit your money.

Table 6-1: Shopping for a Savings Account

	Name of Institution #1:	Name of Institution #2:	Name of Institution #3:
Questions to Ask:			
Is there more than one version of a savings account? If so, what are the differences?			

continued

Table 6-1: Shopping for a Savings Account (continued)

	Name of Institution #1:	Name of Institution #2:	Name of Institution #3:
Is there a minimum deposit to open an account?			
What is the interest rate paid on the account?			
Do yields improve if my balance grows?			
If so, do I earn higher yields on the entire balance or only part of it?			
Is there a monthly maintenance fee?			
If so, is there any way to avoid that fee?			
Is there a fee if my balance drops below the minimum?			
Would the institution consider waiving the fees if I open other accounts here, such as a chequing account?			
Can I write any cheques on this account and if so, what's the fee for writing more than the maximum number in a month?			
What's the fee for using automated teller machines?			

Comparing GICs

As with the other investments we discuss in this chapter, talk to at least three different institutions before you invest in GICs. When you shop around for a GIC, ask the following questions:

- **What's the minimum deposit to open the account?** Usually this amount is $500.

- **What's the interest rate?** What is the compounded annual yield? Interest is the percentage that the bank pays you for allowing them to keep your money. The rate of interest is also called *yield.* Compounded annual yield comes into play if a bank is paying interest monthly, for example. Once the first month's interest is credited to your account, that interest starts earning interest, too, meaning that the compounded annual yield is slightly higher than the interest rate.

- **How often is the interest compounded?** Remember, the more frequently it's compounded, the better it is for you. Continuous compounding is best.

- **Is the interest rate fixed or variable?** Make sure that the institution offers you a way to get current interest rates quickly and easily — by phone, for example.

- **Can you add to your fund at a higher interest rate if the rate goes up while your money is invested?** If the rate goes up substantially, and you can add to your fund, then you can significantly increase your yield.

- **What's the penalty for early withdrawal?** These penalties can wipe out any interest you earn.

- **What happens to the deposit when the GIC matures?** Does the institution roll a matured GIC into a new one of a similar term? Does it mail a cheque? Credit your chequing account?

- **Do they offer market-linked GICs?** Market-linked GICs are indexed (or tied) to the performance of the stock market. Be sure to ask what formula the bank will use to determine performance.

CHAPTER 7
TAKING THE PLUNGE INTO BROKERAGE INVESTMENTS

IN THIS CHAPTER

- Finding a broker
- Buying stocks, bonds, and mutual funds through a broker

In Chapter 4, we offer a short course on the basics of stocks and bonds, the different kinds of securities in each of these broad categories, and the way these instruments fit into an investment plan.

When it comes time to actually make a purchase, a first-time investor understandably can get a little nervous about the details. The purpose of this chapter is to take some of the mystery out of buying stocks, bonds, or mutual funds. Along the way, we alert you to some pitfalls that you want to avoid.

Buying Stocks

The most common way to buy stock is to deal with a broker, which can be either land-based (the kind with folks who work in offices downtown) or in cyberspace (accessed via the Internet).

Choosing a broker

The first big choice you need to make is deciding which kind of broker you are going to deal with: full-service or discount.

If you believe that you are going to need a lot of advice, a full-service broker will probably better serve you. If you are making your own decisions about stocks, by all means use a discount broker. Discount brokers charge much lower commissions than full-service brokers.

Many discount brokers have both electronic and "bricks and mortar" systems of operation. If your discount broker is on the Web, you can enter your order electronically and receive confirmation the same way. Some discount brokers have branch offices where you can sit down and discuss your investment objectives and goals.

Either way, you can obtain commission costs and product information by visiting a discount broker's Web site, by calling their phone number (usually toll-free), or by stopping by the branch office.

In addition to discount commissions, most discount brokers also offer other products and services, such as mutual funds, research reports, bonds, and others.

Full-service brokers are paid by the commissions they earn on buying and selling stocks and other products for clients. This arrangement can lead to a tendency to recommend frequent trading of stocks rather than pursuing a "buy and hold" strategy. This advice can put their interests in conflict with yours. So if you use a full-service broker, avoid miscommunication by making sure that the broker knows that you are not interested in frequent trading but in buying good stocks and holding them for the long term.

You may be better off if you find a good financial adviser to guide you on stock purchases and perhaps on other aspects of your financial program. These advisers often work for a flat fee on an hourly basis.

If you decide to work with a full-service broker, you have to choose a broker one way or another. How do you make this choice? You probably select a broker pretty much the same way you select a doctor, a lawyer, or other professional. You ask people for recommendations. You look in the phone book. You see ads in the newspaper or on television. After you acquire a list of potential brokers, take the process one step further. After you get several names, make some calls.

Call their offices and ask about account minimums and commission costs. Find out how convenient their services are. If you're put on hold for longer than a few minutes or the broker asks to call you back but never does, this individual may not be the broker for you.

Narrow down your choices to two or three brokers and then interview each of them. Make several copies of the worksheet in Table 7-1, and keep them handy when you conduct your final interviews.

Sooner or later, you will get on a mailing list that is sold to brokers. Then you start getting unsolicited calls. All brokers have a good line and can be very persuasive. Our recommendation: Find a financial planner in your area and deal with that person face-to-face. A good financial planner whom you trust can be very helpful to you as you work to achieve your financial goals.

Table 7-1:   Questions to Ask a Prospective Broker

Question	Answer
How long have you been a broker?	
What type of training/ education have you received?	
How much money does it take to open an account (account minimums)?	
What are your commission costs to buy and/or sell stocks?	
What investment strategy do you recommend for a first-time investor?	
Which stocks have you and/or your firm recently recommended?	
How have these stocks performed?	
Can you provide me with two or three professional references?	
a.	
b.	
c.	

Signing a new account agreement form and setting up an account

After you figure out which broker you want to use to place your order, get back in touch with that person.

The broker will ask you to fill out an application, called the *new account agreement form*. You can't avoid filling out this application. No broker can deal with you until you have provided information about yourself and your financial situation and goals. From the start, the broker will need accurate information to process stock purchases and, regrettably but necessarily, to keep Revenue Canada informed about all the money you make from your investments.

The application requires you to provide common personal information such as your name, address, social insurance number, current job (if employed), bank, income, and an estimate of your net worth.

If you are working with a full-service broker, you need to answer some broad questions about your investment goals, your willingness to take risks, and the kinds of stocks you are considering for investment.

Some very personal questions about your finances and goals may puzzle you or even turn you off, but brokers require this information for good reasons. A full-service broker is required by regulation to provide stock advice appropriate to the client's situation. This is often referred to as the "know your client" rule.

There are two other aspects of the customer agreement that you should be aware of. The first is extensive and detailed information about how you will pay for your purchases and what happens if you are late in paying or don't pay at all. This part of the application is complex and legalistic.

We don't want to exaggerate the complexity of the agreement in general. It is long and detailed, but your broker should be willing to answer your questions. The securities industry is closely regulated, and you can be quite sure that the client agreement is not intended to deceive you. It just takes patience to wade through it.

If you can't figure out what some parts of it mean, be persistent in asking your broker to explain the difficult parts. This could be a good test of whether you have picked the right broker. You will have lots of questions all along the way. Don't deal with a broker who doesn't have the time or inclination to work with you.

Make sure that you read and understand the client agreement before you sign it. Don't be rushed into signing it.

Some brokers, especially Internet-based brokers, require that when you establish your account with them, you also set up an account with sufficient funds in it to cover anticipated purchases. The brokerage then pays you interest on the funds you deposit with it.

When you open a typical buy-and-sell brokerage account (called a *cash account*), some brokerage firms allow you to open a separate self-directed *RRSP account* (where you'll hold any investments that you want inside your RRSP) using the same new account form. If you open the cash and RRSP accounts at different times, you'll have to fill out a second form. There is often an annual fee for RRSP accounts.

Placing an order

Placing an order for stocks is simple. You need to know just two things: the name of the stock and the number of shares you want to buy.

If you are dealing with a live broker, the usual process is to place your order by phone. If you are dealing with an Internet broker, the transaction is made on your computer screen and you provide the same information that you would phone in to a broker.

Under federal regulations, the buyer must pay for stock purchases within three business days. This industry rule is called the *three-day settlement*. Brokers are very concerned to see that you pay within this period because they can be penalized or disciplined if payment deadlines are not observed.

After transacting your order, your broker tells you what the total charge is and sends you a written confirmation. (You can also check the Web site for your filled order, or call your broker on the phone.) The charge includes the price of the shares and the broker's commission. You then have three business days to get your payment to the broker. Both discount and full-service brokerages require that money be in the account within three business days. Many investors find it more convenient to have funds in a money market fund at the brokerage before a trade is placed in order to meet the three-day requirement.

Use an overnight delivery service to deliver your payment. Sometimes full-service brokers provide clients with prepaid overnight mailers to use in sending payments. These services almost always deliver cheques in a timely way, and they also have the means to precisely track when and where your payment was delivered.

Finding out about fees

The fees related to the purchase of stocks are few and easy to understand. You'll be required to pay some kind of commission both when you buy and when you sell stocks and small processing fees depending on the type of transaction you require. There's also an administration fee charged on self-directed RRSP accounts. You may also be charged processing fees for some services, like transfers from a cash account to an RRSP account.

The biggest fee is the commission on purchases. Because of the competition from online discount brokers, commissions have been falling. Flat-rate charges in the $28–$40 range are starting to appear at discount brokerages. Rates this low were unknown ten years ago. Full-service brokerages still charge much higher fees. Still, each company determines its fees in a slightly different way, so it pays to shop around. Table 7-2 shows the importance of comparing brokerages.

Some full-service brokers negotiate commissions. Be sure to ask and be sure to take the commissions and other fees into consideration when you select your broker.

Purchasing Bonds

Buying bonds is a lot like buying stocks. You just get in touch with your broker, set up an account, and place your order. If you already have an account with a broker, whether land-based or Internet, you shouldn't have to fill out any additional paperwork to buy a bond. The one account should allow you to purchase stocks, bonds, and mutual funds as well. Unless you are going to concentrate most of your investment money in bonds, there's usually no need to select a broker who specializes in this kind of security.

You do, of course, have to pay for any bonds that you purchase. You pay in the same way and time frame as with stocks (within three days of placing the buying order). Fortunately, you don't get charged much in the way of miscellaneous fees when you buy bonds. These fees vary with the brokerage, but in almost all cases they are very small (sometimes less than $1 per transaction).

Table 7-2: **Fees Differ from Broker to Broker**

Transaction	Brokerage	Number of Shares	Transaction Fee	Per-Share Fee	Total Fee
Purchase XYZ company stock	Broker #1	100	$19.95	$0.25	$34.95
Purchase XYZ company stock	Broker #2	100	$19.95	None	$19.95

Commissions on bonds are about in the same range as those for stocks — high with full-service brokers and lower with discount and Internet brokers. Because investors show much less interest in bonds, competition has not yet brought bond commissions down to the very low levels that are paid for stock transactions on the Internet.

The Internet doesn't have as many Web sites devoted to information about investing in bonds as it does sites about the stock market. There are, however, a couple of outstanding Canadian sites that more than make up for the lack of numbers. For background on bonds, try The Bond Market: A Canadian Perspective, at www.bondcan.com. For information on all types of Government of Canada bonds, check out Canada Investment and Savings at www.cis-pec.gc.ca. For information about bond ratings, go to the Canadian Bond Rating Service at www.cbrs.com or to Dominion Bond Rating Service at www.dbrs.com. Although specific to the U.S. bond market, general information on buying bonds and answers to frequently asked questions about the industry can be had at The Bond Market Association site at www.investinginbonds.com.

Bonds trade on a type of OTC (over-the-counter) market, and most trade without securities symbols you see on securities that are traded on an organized stock exchange, like the Toronto Stock Exchange. Therefore, the investor has to tell the broker the type, how long (time) the investor will hold the bond, and state the investor's risk parametres. Most brokerages (discount and full-service) maintain a bond-trading department in order to meet varied customer needs and preferences.

Purchasing Mutual Funds

When you are ready to invest in mutual funds, you can either work through a broker or, in many cases, you can buy directly from the mutual fund company. Many funds offer a toll-free number for placing orders, and you can buy shares of their funds directly.

Unlike stocks, you don't have to specify the number of shares you want to buy. You tell the fund company or broker that you want to invest a stated amount, and then the fund company or broker tells you how many shares you will get. Also unlike stocks, mutual funds sell partial or fractional shares.

A mutual fund company can't sell you shares of a fund unless you have first received the prospectus for that fund. Whether you call or request the prospectus on the Web, you have to give your name and address. Fund managers need this information data in order to prove that that they have fulfilled their obligation to supply you with a prospectus.

Tip

When you begin to look into mutual funds, pay close attention to those that come in families — preferably big families. The term *family* refers to companies that offer several different kinds of funds. How big is big? Think in terms of ten or more funds. You can spot these families easily by looking at the mutual fund reports in the business section of your daily newspaper. You typically see some kind of headline in the columns followed by a list of funds offered by a particular firm. It's easy to spot the big families at a glance; these include Altamira, Fidelity, Templeton, and Trimark.

Families of funds that charge commissions sometimes provide the opportunity to switch among their funds without paying additional commissions (which can run you about 2% otherwise). You can save considerable money with this option over the long term. Make sure to check out this possibility.

When buying mutual fund shares, you'll face three main types of fees:

- **Management and administration fees.** The mutual fund industry has a standard measurement for both a fund's expenses and its professional management. It's called the *management expense ratio* (MER), which we discuss in Chapter 3. A typical MER will be in the 2% range, and it is subtracted directly from the fund's total assets, thereby reducing your returns.

- **Sales fees.** Unlike the MER, sales fees are not tied to a fund's performance. Also called *loads,* some funds charge these fees when you buy your mutual fund shares (called *front-end loads*). Others charge them when you sell your shares (call *back-end loads*). Some funds charge at both ends. Loads are negotiable depending on the amount being invested and the relationship between the seller and the customer. Front-end loads tend to decrease for larger investments. Back-end loads, sometimes called *redemption fees,* are charged on a declining scale over time. The longer you keep your shares, the lower the fee. As a rule, the fee goes down to 0% after seven years.

- **Trailer fees.** These are commissions paid directly out of a fund's assets to compensate mutual fund brokers for continued service to clients (like you). Although the Ontario Securities Commission requires disclosure of the amount paid in trailer fees in the fund's prospectus, trailer fees are a matter of controversy. Many consider them deferred sales fees and believe they represent a hidden cost, especially since they are also charged to *no-load* funds, which are ostensibly sales fee-free.

No-load funds don't charge front- or back-end loads, but may pay trailer fees from their assets. No-load funds are available in every major fund category. Many investors wonder why they should pay a commission to buy shares of a mutual fund when they can buy a similar fund without a commission. The short answer is that you save money with a no-load fund.

However, the short answer is incomplete. If you are paying a load but are compensated with expert advice at the time you purchase your shares, you will probably reap returns that will make up for the initial sales fee. Also, ask yourself how long you are planning to keep your shares. If you are a long-term investor, you may be able to avoid back-end fees altogether.

Our advice is that you should judge a mutual fund on more than its fees. By reviewing factors like the MER, manager's tenure and performance over time (all of which we explain in Chapter 3), you will make an informed choice that should lead to good returns.

CHAPTER 8

MONITORING YOUR PROGRESS

IN THIS CHAPTER

- How to monitor your investments
- Which indices you need to track
- What to expect from the markets' highs and lows

This chapter tells you how to assess the performance of your investments — or those you plan to buy — relative to their peers. It also provides you with tools to determine how the stock and bond markets, and the mutual funds that invest in them, are doing overall.

Checking Up on Savings Accounts and GICs

In Chapter 2, we qualify these investments as entry-level, or low-complexity, investments. The same holds true for monitoring their progress.

Traditional savings accounts and tiered accounts

Monitoring your savings account or tiered account is a lot like monitoring your chequing account. You receive statements from the institution (like your bank or credit union) that tell you your balance including accrued interest. Many institutions also have a telephone number — often toll-free — that allows you to access balance information by using your account number and your personal code number. In addition, more and more financial institutions have online banking that allows you to access your account information from your computer.

Guaranteed Investment Certificates

When you invest in a Guaranteed Investment Certificate (GIC), you receive an actual document that indicates the principal you invested, the interest rate, the length of time of the investment, and the final amount you will receive. Some institutions include your balance information on the statements you receive from other accounts you have with them, but not all do that.

The most important question with a GIC is what will happen to your money (both the principal and the interest you earn) when the GIC matures. This is your decision. Keep in mind, with GICs, you've agreed to lock in your principal as well as the interest for a specified amount of time. What happens to that money after the term of the GIC is entirely up to you.

Banks and credit unions will generally ask for your *instructions for maturity* when you buy the GIC. You can instruct them to re-invest the money into another GIC, move it into a different investment, place it in a bank account, or have it returned to you. If the GIC is within your RRSP, you will be subject to a federal withholding tax (income tax you pay up front) if you decide to cash it in at maturity instead of reinvesting.

Remember

Most institutions send out a notice a few weeks before your GIC matures. If you want to change your instructions for maturity at that time (or anytime before the maturation date), call your financial institution and let them know.

Looking at Performance: The Indices

An *index* is a statistical yardstick used to gauge the performance of a particular market or group of investments. By tracking average prices or the movement of prices of a group of similar investments, such as small- or large-company stocks or bonds, an index produces a benchmark measure against which you can assess an individual investment's performance.

Think of using an index the same way that you may use a list of comparable home sales when you shop for a house in a neighbourhood. If the list of comparable homes shows you that the average three-bedroom colonial sells for $189,000, you can't expect to buy a similar house for too much less than that. At the same time, you don't want to pay too much more. In the same respect, the benchmarks produced by an index show you a reasonable performance target.

Remember

A *return* is an investment's performance over time. If you're looking at performance for a period of time, say five years, look for an average annual return. If the same mutual fund returned 10% over the course of those five years, its average annual return would be 10%. Its *cumulative return,* which simply totals an investment's performance year after year, would be 50% for those five years.

If an investment's performance over the course of a year is vastly superior or inferior to the appropriate index's return, you'll want to know why. Your investment may be outpacing its peers because it's a lot riskier. A mutual fund, for example, may invest in stocks or bonds that are far riskier than other funds it may resemble. On the other hand, an investment may be lagging its peers simply because it's a poor performer. Bear in mind, however, that you have to build a performance history over time to determine the character of a particular investment. Notice that in Figure 8-1, the mutual fund is performing below average, which may prompt you to sell that investment.

Figure 8-1: A poor performer.

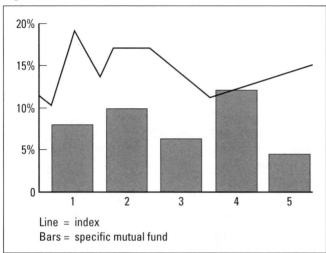

Line = index
Bars = specific mutual fund

The following sections offer a look at the indices that are likely to come in handiest as you try to determine expected performance from your investments.

Start by tracking an index that represents or follows your stock or mutual fund. After you become familiar with that index, pick up another index to follow. Be careful not to follow too many indices, though — it can become confusing and time-consuming.

Canadian Indices

The number of Canadian stock, bond, and mutual fund indices continues to grow, with more specialized indices popping up over time. The ones described in this section are those you'll see on the daily business pages. Just about everyone in the investment world refers to them, and you will too.

The TSE 300 Composite Index

The TSE 300 is the best recognized and most consulted Canadian index. It keeps track of the average performance of 300

Canadian large-company stocks trading on the Toronto Stock Exchange, and is weighted according to market value. An index committee of the TSE reviews the companies periodically and may replace companies for several reasons, including, for example, bankruptcy.

The performance of the 300 stocks is calculated daily, and acts as a daily measure of the market's rise or fall as well as an overall performance figure. These are the numbers you hear reported on the nightly news, see in newspapers, and can view on your computer screen if you log on to a personal finance Web site.

The TSE 300 tells you the average performance of the stocks in the index. This performance is reported as both numbers and percentages. If the TSE goes up, your newspaper might report that "the TSE went up 2 points or 6% today." When the stock market is doing well, the numbers and percentages go up. When it's doing poorly, they go down.

The TSE 300 is divided into 14 industries, and further divided into 40 sub-industries. Here is a list of the 14 main industries, including one of the better-known companies tracked in each:

■ **Metals and Minerals:** Inco Ltd.

■ **Gold and Precious Metals:** Placer Dome Inc.

■ **Oil and Gas:** Imperial Oil Ltd.

■ **Paper and Forest Products:** Abitibi-Consolidated Inc.

■ **Consumer Products:** Maple Leaf Foods Inc.

■ **Industrial Products:** Algoma Steel Inc.

■ **Real Estate:** Trizec Hahn Corporation

■ **Transportation and Environmental Services:** Air Canada

■ **Pipelines:** TransCanada PipeLines Inc.

■ **Utilities:** BCE Inc.

■ **Communications and Media:** CanWest Global Communications Corp.

■ **Merchandising:** Sears Canada Inc.

■ **Financial Services:** Bank of Montreal

■ **Conglomerates:** Canadian Pacific Ltd.

(Source: *TSE Index Services*)

The TSE 35

Another heavily quoted Canadian stock index is the TSE 35. Started in 1987, the TSE 35 follows the 35 top-performing Canadian large-company stocks trading on the Toronto Stock Exchange. Some of the companies we used as examples above, like Alcan, TransCanada PipeLines Inc., and the Bank of Montreal, are also tracked by the TSE 35. While both the TSE 300 and the TSE 35 rise and fall daily, the TSE 35 tracks a much narrower range of companies, and is not as useful for investors who want a general benchmark against which to gauge their own stock's performance.

Scotia Capital Markets Universe Bond Index

If you're invested in the Canadian bond market, you won't be able to track the performance of your investments using a stock index like the TSE 300. You have to consult an index designed specifically to track bonds. In Canada, Scotia Capital Markets maintains the best-known bond index.

According to their own information sheets, Scotia Capital Markets would like its index to "reflect performance of the broad 'Canadian Bond Market' in a manner similar to the way the TSE 300 represents the Canadian equity market."

Begun in 1979, the universe bond index comprises more than 900 issues, including Government of Canada, provincial, municipal, and corporate bonds. You'll find the Scotia Capital Markets Universe Bond Index reported in daily newspapers alongside the major stock indices. The bond index is similarly calculated to reflect both number and percentage changes.

The U.S. Indices

While the Canadian indices will be most useful to you as an investor, it's also a fact that the American economy and its stock markets are considered the world leaders. Individual investors, business people, financial advisors and mutual fund managers all keep their eye on the performance of key U.S. indices when assessing their own progress in the market. You're sure to recognize at least one of the following key U.S. indices.

The Standard & Poor's 500

Also called the S&P 500, the Standard & Poor's index has become the dominant benchmark in U.S. investing in recent years. The S&P 500 tracks the performance of 500 stocks, comprising of 400 industrial companies, 40 utilities, 20 transportation companies, and 40 financial firms.

The S&P 500 is home to some of the hottest stocks of the late 1990s, including U.S.-based AOL and Dell, the latter of which gave investors an unrivaled 79.7% average annual return, not for a day, not for a month, but for ten years. With so much fanfare, the S&P has become the index to beat for many mutual fund managers. Outperforming it is cause for celebration.

The Dow Jones Industrial Average

The Dow Jones Industrial Average (DJIA) tracks the performance of 30 companies that are among the largest companies and some of the most venerable stocks the U.S. stock market has to offer. If you own one of these stocks, such as Exxon or IBM, you'll want to know how your stock is faring compared to the average.

The results of the Dow are reported daily in newspapers across Canada, the U.S., and the world, as well as on news and financial Web sites. The results, which tell readers the average performance of the stocks in the index, are reported as both numbers and percentages. If the Dow goes up, your newspaper might report that "the Dow was up 4 points or 10% today." When the index goes up, investors are actively buying stocks and the stocks covered by the index are going up in value.

The Dow Jones is known all over the world, and serves as a daily report on how well the powerful U.S. economy is doing. After falling behind somewhat in the esteem of some critics for shying away from tracking high-tech stocks, the index has very recently been updated. While it still tracks the same number of companies — 30 to be exact — that number now includes computer giant Microsoft and retail giant Home Depot. It's important to look at the Dow relative to its index peers to get a sense about whether certain slices of the stock market are faring better or worse than others.

The Dow Jones Industrial Average is price-weighted — giving companies with a higher stock price more weight regardless of their size. Because of price-weighting, one company's stock can pull the index up or down significantly, even if that direction doesn't reflect the performance of the majority of the index's stocks. That price-weighting doesn't mean you can ignore the DJIA, which follows the performance of giants such as AT&T and General Electric, but you should understand how the average is determined.

The Nasdaq Composite Index

The Nasdaq is another widely quoted U.S. index. It is some-times seen as a competitor to the S&P, but the Nasdaq Composite is actually very different. For starters, Nasdaq measures the stock performance of 5,500 companies, nearly half of them in the telecommunications and high-tech arena, and all of them found in the Nasdaq market. The index includes giant U.S. companies like Apple, Intel, MCI Communications, Cisco, Oracle, Sun Microsystems, and Netscape.

As a result, the Nasdaq index is a good deal more volatile than, for example, the Dow Jones Industrial Average and, perhaps, the stock market at large. It's also home to some of the bigger success stories of the 1990s, many of which are technology firms. The higher the potential for return an investment has, the more the risk it carries.

Just like the Dow Industrial Average and the S&P 500, the Nasdaq Composite gives the average performance of the stocks in the index both as numbers and percentages. If the Nasdaq goes up, your newspaper might report that "the Nasdaq was up 1 point or 3% today."

The Wilshire 5000

Want a good look at how the overall U.S. stock market is doing? The Wilshire 5000 tracks a huge universe of stocks — in fact, it lists almost every publicly listed stock, including those listed on the New York Stock Exchange, the American Stock Exchange, and the Nasdaq Composite. That's a pretty definitive look at the large-, medium-, and small-company stock markets.

This is not a must-read index, especially on a daily basis, but it is an index investors want to at least know about and have the option of viewing once in a while. It's the largest index going. It gives an investor a broad sense of how the U.S. stock market is faring overall and in which direction stocks are headed. More mutual funds have also started investing in stocks listed in the Wilshire 5000, which gives investors total U.S. stock exposure.

Remembering That Performance is Relative

Everything is relative, regardless of which investment performances you're measuring. What may have been great performance a year ago may be considered good, bad, or indifferent today, depending on how the particular market you're invested in is doing.

Warning

Unless you have evidence of other negative indicators, don't knee-jerk into selling an investment just because its performance lags behind an index one year. You're investing for the long term. What's underperforming its index this year may well bounce back next year.

The trick to using indices is to be able to definitively tell how well the performance of your investments stacks up against that of their peers in the market you're in. With that know-how, you can answer questions like: Is this stock's performance average? Is this mutual fund's performance above average? Is this bond's performance poor?

How does your performance compare with the indices? Although you don't want to be 50% or more off the indices or benchmarks for your investments, lagging 10% to 20% behind is nothing to sneeze at. For example, if in 1998 your investments came in 20% under the TSE 300's 28% performance, you would have reported more than a 22% return. Could you live with that? You should be happy to. With a 20% return, you'll more than double your initial investment in four years. These are the kinds of years you come to live for as an investor. And you'll be glad you built a portfolio rather than investing in just one or two stocks that may have entirely missed this increase in value.

Looking Rationally at Market Highs and Lows

You're investing hard-earned money, so you want to enjoy a sense of comfort and confidence in your investments' potential to perform as expected *over time*. We emphasize the phrase *over time* because chasing short-term performance can drive you crazy.

Investments can look mighty risky if you track their performance every day. In contrast, risk tends to flatten out a bit if you look at it year to year. In fact, since the late 1920s, few classes of investments have lost money over a ten-year period. Of course, some individual investments have lost money, but the general rule applies: Holding on to investments for a longer period of time will reduce your exposure to losses.

Do you want to avoid undue risk? Invest for the long term — or, at the very least, five years. If you need to tap your investments earlier than that, stick to shorter-term cash equivalents, such as money market mutual funds (which invest in high-grade bonds with shorter maturities) and guaranteed investment certificates.

Learning how to gauge the market is different from thinking you can predict the market. No one — not even the most savvy broker — knows with any real certainty how well or how poorly the market will fare in the future.

Reaching Your Goals

After you start investing, monitor your progress to ensure that you're on track. Make the anniversary of your first investment your day of financial reckoning (or at least that month).

When the day arrives, sit down and take an earnest look at what you're investing in, how much you're investing, whether or not your goals have shifted or changed completely, and whether or not you're saving enough (and earning enough on your investments) to reach your goals.

The ultimate measure of your portfolio isn't whether or not you're beating the benchmarks. It's whether or not you're reaching your goals. Are you? For example, if you determined at the outset that you needed to invest $500 a month and earn an average annual return of 9%, are you hitting your goal?

If you're meeting or beating your goals, you're in great shape. If you're not, identify what's wrong. Maybe you're not investing enough. You may have to pay off some bills so that you can find more money in your household budget to invest. Or you may find that your RRSP needs greater funding, so you have to increase the percentage of your pay you contribute each week or month.

To ensure that your investment plan is a workhorse that's pulling its weight, feed it. As you get raises at work, or come into "found" money — maybe a small inheritance, a bonus at work, or a tax refund — consider investing some or even all of these funds in your portfolio.

Knowing When to Sell

Of course, maybe one or more of your investments isn't performing up to your standards. This kind of letdown happens to the best of us, and you can count on a disappointment once or twice in your investment life. When underperformance hits home with one of your investments, take a deep breath and try to figure out what's happening.

Figuring out how long to hold on to an investment that isn't producing any growth is a challenge. You have to first determine what is keeping the investment on the rocks. The following sections offer a look at why an investment may be underperforming.

When you sell a stock, bond, or mutual fund, make sure that you find a suitable replacement and don't leave the cash lying in your chequing account, where it may be pilfered away by life's daily expenses.

Is the economy the reason for your investment's slump?

Is the entire market taking its lumps? If so, your investment isn't immune. If one or more sectors of the stock market are taking a licking, consider the impact to your stock, bond, or mutual fund. A sluggish economy, or one that is in retreat, can play havoc with investments. Investments are long-term endeavours. Don't sell just because of an economic downturn. You'll take a loss.

An economic downturn can create a buying opportunity if it sends the price of stocks spiraling downward.

Is your stock falling behind?

If a stock is struggling, look at the company. Forget about what's happened to date for a moment. If you discovered the company again today, would you buy it? Do some future analysis on the company's prospects. Don't let your answer be clouded by negative feelings about the past few months or years. If you bought the stock because you believed that the company was well positioned for a turn-around due to new and competitive products or services, sales, profits, or other facets of its financial position, hang on a bit more. The last thing you want to do is take a loss on a stock that may turn around a few days or months after you give it the boot.

At the same time, if you decide you wouldn't buy the stock again today, or some of the economic reasons that attracted you to the stock in the first place haven't panned out, selling is okay.

Is your bond slipping behind?

If a bond is doing poorly, maybe because interest rates have risen (bond prices move in reverse of interest rates), ask yourself what cost you can expect from hanging on to the bond until maturity. Compare that expense with what it will cost you to sell the bond. If interest rates jump substantially, say, to 15%, and you're hanging on to a bond paying 4%, you might well be better off selling the older issue and buying a new bond.

Is your mutual fund fumbling?

If your mutual fund isn't performing up to snuff, look at the fund manager's style. If the stock market is growth-oriented and your manager is a value manager who looks for bargains, you may be wise to hang on. Value-style investing comes in and out of favour, and you wouldn't want to miss the upside. Of course, if an inept mutual fund manager is the only reason you can find for the lagging performance, you can sell. Try to wait until a fund's performance has been impaired for at least two years in order to avoid unnecessary losses.

CHAPTER 9
NOW WHAT?

IN THIS CHAPTER

- Determining your comfort level
- Diversifying your investment approach
- Finding out what you need to know about taxes

Right about now, you're probably feeling some sense of satisfaction. You've begun the enviable journey of building an investment plan and realizing your financial goals. Beyond the load of information you've absorbed already, some additional common-sense concepts can make your investing experience more productive and less mysterious. A few tricks of the trade also can help you become a more effective investor by guiding you around some of the pitfalls that trip up even the most earnest and dedicated investors.

Starting and Staying with a Diversified Investment Approach

The goal of diversification is to minimize risk. Instead of putting your eggs in one basket by investing every dime you have in one stock, one bond, or one mutual fund, you should diversify.

Diversification is a strategy for investing in a wide array of investments that ideally move slightly out of step with each other. For example, an investment in an international mutual fund might be doing poorly while an investment in a Canadian equity mutual fund is doing well. By investing in different sectors of the investment markets, you create a balanced portfolio. Parts of that portfolio should zig when other sections zag.

Table 9-1 shows the power of diversification by examining how three different diversified portfolios of money markets, bonds, and stocks can fare over time. The table also gives you a concrete idea of the investments that should go in a portfolio based on your own tolerance for risk. They're also a good way for you to measure whether your own portfolio is diverse enough for your own tolerance for risk or loss.

Table 9-1: Three Models of Diversification

	Lower Risk/ Return Portfolio	Moderate Risk/ Return Portfolio	Higher Risk/ Return Portfolio
Makeup	20% money markets, 40% bonds, 40% stocks	20% money markets, 30% bonds, 50% stocks	20% money markets, 0% bonds, 80% stocks
Return for best year	22.8%	28.1%	35%
Return for worst year	–6.7%	–13.4%	–19.6%
Average annual return	9%	10.1%	10.9%

It's important to determine the percentage of stocks, bonds, and cash you want in your portfolio. In the stock and bond categories (or mutual funds that invest in these assets), it's also important not to load up on any one sector of the economy. So steer clear of the temptation to invest in three technology mutual funds, four Internet stocks, or six junk bonds — even if they're paying more than other investments.

The saying "no pain, no gain" also applies to the investment experience. You can avoid the prospect of experiencing any pain at all by investing only in Canada Savings Bonds and GICs that are federally insured. The price to be paid for that strategy: You may never lose money in the traditional sense, but you never gain much either, which means that you can still fall behind. You also run the risk of falling behind because of inflation, which eat ups about 1-3% of your purchasing power each year. If you only earn 4% or 5% a year on your savings or investments, you'll have a hard time preserving the capital you have, let alone growing it.

Developing a Dollar Cost Averaging Plan

No one can afford to have an investing plan forgotten or relegated to the back burner. You need to set up a plan for making set, regular investments. This way, you ensure that your money is working for you even if your best intentions are diverted.

Dollar cost averaging is a way to ensure that you make fixed investments every month or quarter, regardless of other distractions in your life. Dollar cost averaging is a simple concept: You invest a specified dollar amount each month without concern about the price per share or cost of the bond. The market is *fluid* — the price of your investment moves up and down — so you end up buying shares when they're inexpensive, some when they're expensive, and some when they're somewhere in between. Because of the commission cost to buy small amounts of stocks or bonds, dollar cost averaging is better suited for buying mutual funds.

In addition to helping you overcome procrastination about saving for investments, dollar cost averaging can help you sidestep some of the anxiety many first-time investors feel about starting to invest in a market that can seem too overheated or risky. With set purchases each month or quarter, you buy shares of your chosen investments regardless of how the market is doing.

Dollar cost averaging isn't statistically the most lucrative way to invest. Because markets rise more often than they decline, you're better off saving up your money and buying stocks, bonds, or mutual funds when they hit rock bottom. But dollar cost averaging is the most disciplined and reliable way to invest. Consider this: If you set up a dollar cost averaging plan now, then in 10, 20, or 30 years, you'll have invested every month in between and accumulated a pretty penny in the interim.

Most mutual funds let you start out on a dollar cost averaging plan (often called pre-authorized contribution or PAC plans for accounts inside your RRSP) for as little as $50 or $100 a month. The only catch is that you have to sign up to allow the fund to take the money from your chequing account each month. To find out if the funds you're interested in offer the service, look for the information in their prospectuses or call their toll-free shareholder services phone number.

Investing with Your Eye on Taxes

Unfortunately, with investing, as with just about any other activity that generates income, gains are taxable. The federal government collects all income tax for itself and on behalf of the provinces, except in Quebec, where the provincial government collects its own income tax. As a rule, provincial income tax is calculated as a percentage of your federal income tax rate.

The fact that you will pay combined federal and provincial income tax on your investments should not deter you from trying to invest successfully. A good investor will come out ahead in the end. But you should realize now that you will pay taxes on investment gains. Consider the following tax implications for investments *outside* your RRSP:

Savings accounts

Gains on simple savings accounts and tiered savings accounts are taxed as income. Banks and financial institutions report these gains to Revenue Canada, just as all investment gains are reported.

GICs

The interest you earn on GICs must be declared as taxable income, and will be fully taxed on an annual basis. If, for example, your GIC is locked in for five years, that means you will pay tax each of those years — even if you haven't yet received any of the interest.

Mutual funds

With mutual funds, unfortunately, you have to pay tax each year on the interest and capital gains that the fund distributes to each of its shareholders. You also have to pay taxes on your own gains when you sell shares — another reason for a long-term buy-and-hold strategy.

Stocks

With stocks, you don't pay taxes on your gains until you sell your shares — a feature that fans of stock investing say is a clear advantage in the long run. The downside, however, is that when you do cash in shares down the road, your tax bracket or the tax rate may have increased.

Bonds

Price appreciation (if any) on a bond — whether it is a government or corporate bond — is taxable when the bond matures as a capital gain (you will pay tax on 75% of your capital gains annually). If your bond loses value, that loss is deemed a *capital gains loss*. You can apply that loss against other capital gains you report to Revenue Canada.

The interest you earn on a bond is fully taxable annually. That rule applies even to compounded Canada Savings Bonds, where the interest is reinvested yearly, meaning you'll pay tax on interest you haven't yet received.

Tax-deferred investing with RRSPs

As Canadians, we have a very powerful tax-deferral tool in the form of RRSPs. Maxing out your contributions to your registered retirement savings plan really does boil down to a choice of paying yourself or paying Revenue Canada.

As we discussed in Chapter 3, the benefits of investing within an RRSP are twofold: First, all the contributions you make within your RRSP are tax-deductible — in other words, these contributions, up to the allowable limit, become an immediate deduction from your taxable income. Second, the government defers the tax bill for any gains you make on those investments, be they interest, capital gains, or dividends, until you cash in your RRSP.

As discussed in Chapter 3, even after you turn 69, the tax-deferral power of your RRSP will keep working for you. How? You will have the opportunity to convert your RRSP into a registered retirement income fund (RRIF) and withdraw your funds over time rather than in a lump sum. You'll pay less this way, since the government charges less up-front income tax (called withholding tax) on smaller withdrawals. On top of that, the government gives you a *pension income credit* up to $1,000 annually, which reduces the amount of tax you owe for income you receive from qualifying pension income including RRSP funds.

Because interest-bearing investments are fully taxed at your *marginal tax rate* (the rate at which you are taxed on your last earned dollar of a given tax year), many investment advisers suggest these as your first choice to go inside an RRSP. Since capital gains are taxed at a lower rate (only 75% of the gain is added to your overall taxable income), these might be investments to keep outside your RRSP. Dividend-bearing investments from shares in Canadian equities are also taxed at a lower rate. That's because dividends represent a corporation's after-tax profits. To avoid double taxation, the federal government provides some tax relief in the form of a *dividend tax credit,* which reduces the rate at which your dividends from Canadian corporations will be taxed.

Calculating the dividend tax credit is a bit confusing (especially for residents of Quebec, who follow a different formula). For non-Quebec residents, you begin by *grossing up* (multiply upward) the amount of dividends you've received by 25%. Then you calculate federal income tax on that amount. Finally, you subtract the dividend tax credit (which is 13.33% of the grossed-up dividend) from the income tax you've calculated. In the end, you'll see that dividends are taxed at a lower rate than regular income. For those who can't stomach the calculations, keep in mind that dividend-paying Canadian corporations will send you a statement showing the grossed-up amount, as well as the dividend tax credit.

The price you pay for tapping your retirement accounts early

Do not take money out of your RRSP on a whim, say, when you're changing jobs or feel the need for an extravagant vacation. If you make the withdrawal anyway and you're not age yet age 69, the money is considered income and is taxed as such by Revenue Canada at your marginal tax rate. You'll also lose the tax-sheltered earning potential that the money bought you inside the plan.

Income tax on RRSP withdrawals is levied immediately when you take the money out. This way, the government gets its money up front, rather than waiting for you to file your tax return. This manner of extracting income tax is called a withholding tax, and is based on the amount you withdraw. As of the 1999 tax year, if you take $5,000 out of your RRSP, you'll be charged 10% withholding tax (unless you live in

Quebec, where you'll have to pay more — 21% — since the province levies its own withholding tax). Between $5,000 and $15,000, that tax jumps to 20% (30% for residents of Quebec), and again to 30% for withdrawals over $15,000 (35% for residents of Quebec).

Since the withholding tax may not match the amount of tax you actually owe on the money you've withdrawn, you will still have to reckon with Revenue Canada at tax time. Depending on your tax bracket, that will either mean paying more when you file your tax return, or, in some cases, getting a rebate for overpayment.

Revenue Canada lets you borrow money from your RRSP for two specific purposes: a first-time home purchase (through what's called the Home Buyers' Plan or HBP); and post-secondary education (via the Lifelong Learning plan or LLP). In both cases, the money coming out of your RRSP will not be subject to the withholding tax. However, there are specific rules governing when you must pay it back.

Before you borrow any money from your RRSP through the HBP or LLP, take into account the loss of tax-sheltered income growth you will suffer because of these withdrawals. In other words, even though you aren't paying any interest on the loan from your RRSP (as opposed to a traditional mortgage or student loan), you still pay indirectly. Depending on the amount and the length of time the money is out of your RRSP, this indirect loss of income growth could ultimately make a traditional bank loan the smarter choice.

CLIFFSNOTES REVIEW

Use this CliffsNotes Review to practise what you've learned in this book and to build your confidence for making your first investment. After you work through the review questions, some possible scenarios, and the fun and useful projects, you're well on your way to achieving your goal of becoming a successful first-time investor.

Q&A

1. What is a money market fund?_____
_____

2. If you feel comfortable with more risky investments, what mutual fund type may be right for you?

   a. Balanced funds

   b. Equity income funds

   c. Aggressive growth funds

3. An established, old company usually pays dividends

   a. Regularly

   b. Not at all

   c. Infrequently

4. What does the term "bear market" mean?_____
_____

5. If you want to choose tax-smart investments outside your RRSP, you may choose to invest in

   a. GICs

   b. Canadian stocks

   c. A savings account

6. At what age can you make your last RRSP contribution?

   a. The year you turn 60
   b. The year you turn 69
   c. The year you turn 70

7. What four things should first-time investors NOT do?

   1. _____
   2. _____
   3. _____
   4. _____

8. What are three of the indices used to measure stock performance?

   1. _____
   2. _____
   3. _____

9. In most cases, if you withdraw money from your RRSP before your retirement, you will have to pay:

Answers: (1) A money market fund is a mutual fund that invests in short-term low-risk, stable investments. It is not CDIC-insured, but is extremely safe since many of its investments, like T-bills, are guaranteed by the federal government. Money market funds are one of the most popular types of mutual funds. (2) c. (3) a. (4) A bear market is a market in which stock prices drop 20% or more from their previous highs. (5) b. — Dividends from your shares in a Canadian corporation will be taxable at a lower rate because of the federal government's dividend tax credit, while interest on GICs and savings accounts is fully taxed. (6) b. (7) Invest for the short term; speculate or choose risky investments; choose only one type of investment; neglect to do research. (8) TSE 300 Composite Index, TSE 35, Dow Jones Industrial Average. (9) Withholding tax.

Scenario

1. You want to invest for retirement, and you and your spouse have a combined income of $100,000, $80,000 of which you earn. You want to continue investing in your RRSP, but you want to avoid paying high taxes when you withdraw that money at retirement. You choose a _____.

2. You just graduated from university, and your aunt has given you $200 in Canada Savings Bonds. You need money for a new printer for your computer, but also want to start a nest egg. Your best move is to _____
_____.

3. The used car you bought five years ago is starting to show signs of age. You've been saving money in a savings account for major future purchases. Your mechanic has told you that the car will last just another two or three years. The money in your savings account isn't enough for a down payment on another car, but could be if it earned more interest. Two of the best investment vehicles to move your money into are_____
_____.

Answers: (1) Spousal RRSP. You set up this plan in your spouse's name, and you put some (or all) of your contribution into it, creating two income streams at retirement. Since the spousal RRSP is registered to your spouse, who earns only $20,000 in this example, those funds will be taxed at a lower rate when withdrawn. (2) Hold the bonds until maturity because they will be worth more then than the face value now. (3) A GIC or money market fund because they tend to earn more interest than a standard savings account.

Consider This

■ Did you know that some stocks have a dividend reinvestment plan (DRIP)? Some stocks can be set up to automatically reinvest any dividends toward additional shares of that stock. This plan can save on brokerage and other fees.

■ Did you know that starting to invest even a small amount when you are in your 20s can make a significant difference for your retirement funds? Due to compound interest, people who start investing even a $100 a month at age 25 stand to gain considerably when they retire at 60 or 65. People who start to invest the same amount at 35 or 40 can't earn as much due to fewer years of interest.

Practice Projects

1. Investigate different interest rates at banks, trusts, and credit unions. Get information from several different banks and credit unions for six-month, one-year, and two-year GICs. Compare the rates and then decide which is the best option for you.

2. Look through business and financial magazines, such as *Canadian Business, Financial Post Magazine, Report on Business Magazine, IE: Money, Money Sense, Profit, Fortune,* and *Business Week.* Find a few companies that sound like potential investments; research them by using *The Investment Reporter, Investor's Digest of Canada, Financial Post Investment Reports, Blue Book of Stock Reports,* or the U.S. publication *Value Line.* Do the company reports present a different profile from what the articles led you to believe? Which research tool was most useful? Would you invest in any of these companies?

3. Look at your long-term retirement goals. Do you know how much you'll need to retire? What are you doing now to achieve your goals? Research the different types of RRSPs and analyze which is best for you. Are you maximizing your contributions? Are you informed and confident enough to set up a self-directed RRSP?

CLIFFSNOTES RESOURCE CENTRE

The learning doesn't need to stop here. CliffsNotes Resource Centre shows you the best of the best — links to the best investing information in print and online. And don't think that this is all we've prepared for you; we've put all kinds of pertinent information at www.cliffsnotes.com. Look for all the great resources at your favourite bookstore or local library and on the Internet. When you're online, make your first stop www.cliffsnotes.com, where you'll find more incredibly useful information about investing. Happy hunting!

Books

This CliffsNotes book is one of the many great books on investing published by CDG Books Inc., a division of IDG Books Worldwide, Inc. So if you want some great next-step books, check out these other publications:

CliffsNotes Investing in Mutual Funds for Canadians, by John Craig and Juliette Fairley, gives you a more in-depth look at investing in the world of mutual funds. CDG Books Canada, Inc., $8.99.

CliffsNotes Investing in the Stock Market for Canadians, by Marguerite Pigeon and C. Edward Gilpatric, helps you further improve your investing prowess with specific information about investing in stocks. CDG Books Canada, Inc., $8.99.

Investing Online For Dummies, 2nd Edition, by Kathleen Sindell, helps you unlock all the investing resources and capabilities available in the vast world of cyberspace. CDG Books Canada, Inc., $35.99.

Investing For Dummies, 2nd Edition, by Eric Tyson, provides tips and hints about investing that can turn you from a first-timer into a power investor. CDG Books Canada, Inc., $27.99.

Mutual Funds For Dummies, 2nd Edition, by Eric Tyson, enlightens you with over two decades of the author's mutual fund knowledge. Check out the sample portfolios for ideas on your own mutual fund investments. CDG Books Canada, Inc., $26.99

It's easy to find books published and distributed by CDG Books Canada, Inc. including all of the popular lines from IDG Books Worldwide, Inc. You can find them in your favourite bookstores near you and on the Internet. There are four Web sites that you can use to read about our entire line of books:

- www.cdgbooks.com
- www.cliffsnotes.com
- www.dummies.com
- www.idgbooks.com

Internet

Check out the following Web sites for more information about mutual funds, stocks, bonds, real estate, savings accounts, RRSPs, and more:

Canada NewsWire Ltd., www.newswire.ca and **Canadian Corporate News,** www.cdn-news.com are two places to keep track of news on the companies you invest in. At both sites, you'll find up-to-date press releases from the corporate world as well as the federal government.

Canadian Bond Rating Service (CBRS), www.cbrs.com and **Dominion Bond Rating Service (DBRS),** www.dbrs .com have both been in the bond-rating service since the 1970s. Both are independent: They aren't affiliated with any securities seller. So the credibility of the research and ratings is beyond question. At each Web site, you can read up on how the various ratings systems work or go straight to the actual ratings for Government of Canada, provincial, commercial paper, or corporate bonds.

Canadian Deposit Insurance Corporation (CDIC), www. cdic.ca has the final word on which of your investments are insured by the federal government.

i|money, www.imoney.com is a diverse and informative personal finance site with information on just about every money-related topic Canadians could hope for, including up-to-date stock quotes and interest rate postings.

Investment Funds Institute of Canada (IFIC), www. mutfunds.com/ific is a good place to start when considering investing in mutual funds. IFIC's site includes everything from a glossary of terms to the latest statistics on the Canadian mutual fund industry.

Revenue Canada, www.rc.gc.ca keeps a very extensive site, with information on taxation, downloadable fact sheets, forms, interpretation bulletins, and other documents, as well as links upon links to other governmental and non-governmental sites where you will find answers to your investment questions.

SEDAR, www.sedar.com is the electronic filing site maintained by the Canadian Securities Administrators (CSA) — the association that represents the provincial and territorial securities commissions. At SEDAR, you'll find profiles and other securities-related information for many of the public companies traded on the Canadian stock exchanges.

Send Us Your Favourite Tips

In your quest for learning, have you ever experienced that sublime moment when you figure out a trick that saves time or trouble? Perhaps you realized you were taking ten steps to accomplish something that could have taken two. Or you found a little-known workaround that gets great results. If you've discovered a useful tip that helped you budget more effectively and you'd like to share it, the CliffsNotes staff would love to hear from you. Go to our Web site at www.cliffs-notes.com and click the Talk to Us button. If we select your tip, we may publish it as part of *CliffsNotes Daily,* our exciting, free e-mail newsletter. To find out more or to subscribe to a newsletter, go to www.cliffsnotes.com on the Web.

INDEX

COMING SOON FROM CLIFFSNOTES

Online Shopping

HTML

Choosing a PC

Beginning Programming

Careers

Windows 98 Home Networking

eBay Online Auctions

PC Upgrade and Repair

Business

Microsoft Word 2000

Microsoft PowerPoint 2000

Finance

Microsoft Outlook 2000

Digital Photography

Palm Computing

Investing

Windows 2000

Online Research

CDG
BOOKS
CANADA

COMING SOON FROM CLIFFSNOTES
Buying and Selling on eBay

Have you ever experienced the thrill of finding an incredible bargain at a specialty store or been amazed at what people are willing to pay for things that you might toss in the garbage? If so, then you'll want to learn about eBay — the hottest auction site on the Internet. And CliffsNotes *Buying and Selling on eBay* is the shortest distance to eBay proficiency. You'll learn how to:

■ Find what you're looking for, from antique toys to classic cars

■ Watch the auctions strategically and place bids at the right time

■ Sell items online at the eBay site

■ Make the items you sell attractive to prospective bidders

■ Protect yourself from fraud

Here's an example of how the step-by-step CliffsNotes learning process simplifies placing a bid at eBay:

1. Scroll to the Web page form that is located at the bottom of the page on which the auction item itself is presented.

2. Enter your registered eBay username and password and enter the amount you want to bid. A Web page appears that lets you review your bid before you actually submit it to eBay. After you're satisfied with your bid, click the Place Bid button.

3. Click the Back button on your browser until you return to the auction listing page. Then choose View⤵Reload (Netscape Navigator) or View⤵Refresh (Microsoft Internet Explorer) to reload the Web page information. Your new high bid appears on the Web page, and your name appears as the high bidder.